# Continuity of life

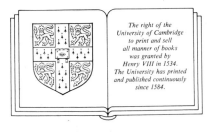

The right of the
University of Cambridge
to print and sell
all manner of books
was granted by
Henry VIII in 1534.
The University has printed
and published continuously
since 1584.

CAMBRIDGE UNIVERSITY PRESS

*Cambridge*
*London   New York   New Rochelle*
*Melbourne   Sydney*

Published by the Press Syndicate of the University of Cambridge
The Pitt Building, Trumpington Street, Cambridge CB2 1RP
32 East 57th Street, New York, NY 10022, USA
296 Beaconsfield Parade, Middle Park, Melbourne 3206, Australia

First published 1984
Printed in Great Britain at the University Press, Cambridge

Library of Congress catalogue card number: 84-1836

*British Library cataloguing in publication data*

Continuity of life: growth, reproduction and
    development—(Advanced biology alternative
    learning project; unit 4)
    1. Growth
    I. Advanced Biology Alternative Learning Project
    II. Series
    574.3'1   QH491
    ISBN 0 521 28826 6

# Contents

# Acknowledgements

**Figures:** 1, extract from data on p.112 of Revised Nuffield O-level text 4, *The Perpetuation of Life*, pub. July 1975, Longman and courtesy of the Nuffield Foundation; 2, E. Ashby (1938) *School Science Review*, **19**, 409–18; 3, 11, 14, 15, 41, 42, 43, 50, 53, 92, 95, 97, 104, 105, 118, 119, 120, 121, 122, 124, 126, 127, 129, 130, 132, 133, 134, 136, Biophoto Associates; 6, M. Balls & P.M. Godsell (1973) *Journal of Biological Education*, no. 7; 16, modified from diagram 33b on p.78 of *Organisms and Population*, Nuffield Advanced Science, pub. July 1974, Longman and courtesy of the Nuffield Foundation; 17, 19, 20, redrawn and adapted from illustrations a, b and c from page 80 of *Organisms and Population*, Nuffield Advanced Science, pub. July 1974, Longman and courtesy of the Nuffield Foundation; 23, adapted from fig 85 from p.170 of Nuffield Advanced Science *Study Guide*, pub. July 1974, Longman and courtesy of the Nuffield Foundation; 25, adapted from D.O. Hall & S.E. Hawkins (1975) *Laboratory Manual of Cell Biology*; 28, 29, graphs on pages 249 and 250 from Nuffield Advanced Science *Study Guide*, pub. July 1974, Longman and courtesy of the Nuffield Foundation and J.M. Tanner; 45, courtesy of Philip Harris Biological Ltd.; 55, J.M. Tanner (1962) *Growth at Adolescence*, Blackwell and J.Z. Young (1982) *An Introduction to the Study of Man*, Oxford University Press; 70, 78, A.G. Clegg & P.C. Clegg (1975) *Biology of the Mammal*, 4th ed., William Heinemann Medical Books; 71, 72, from *The Birth Atlas*, Maternity Center Association, New York; 76, P.J. Marshall & G.M. Hughes (1980) *Physiology of Mammals and Other Vertebrates*, Cambridge University Press; 90, D. Harrison (1971) *Advanced Biology Notes*, Macmillan, London & Basingstoke; 91, Maud Jepson (1938) *Biological Drawings*, John Murray; 93, 107, courtesy of C. Dodds & J.B. Hurn; 111, 112, courtesy of D.G. Mackean; 123, 128, C.J. Clegg & Gene Cox (1978) *Anatomy and Activities of Plants*, John Murray; 140, D. Harrison (1975) *Patterns in Biology*, Edward Arnold and courtesy of Dr R.F.O. Kemp; 141, 142, 145, 162, reprinted with permission from J.W. Kimball © 1965 *Biology*, Addison–Wesley, Reading Ma.; 152, courtesy of the Trustees of the British Museum (Natural History); 154, M.D. Robson & A.G. Morgan (1980) *Biology Today*, Macmillan; 156, graph on page 251 from Nuffield Advanced Science *Study Guide*, pub. July 1974, Longman and courtesy of the Nuffield Foundation; 157, 163, courtesy of Professor V.B. Wigglesworth.

**Examination questions:** By permission of the University of Cambridge Local Examinations Syndicate, the University of London University Entrance and School Examinations Council and the Southern Universities Joint Board.

# Preface

The Inner London Education Authority's Advanced Biology Alternative Learning (ABAL) project has been developed as a response to changes which have taken place in the organisation of secondary education and the curriculum. The project is the work of a group of biology teachers seconded from ILEA secondary schools. ABAL began in 1978 and since then has undergone extensive trials in schools and colleges of further education. The materials have been produced to help teachers meet the needs of new teaching situations and provide an effective method of learning for students.

Teachers new to A-level teaching or experienced teachers involved in reorganisation of schools due to the changes in population face many problems. These include the sharing of staff and pupils between existing schools and the variety of backgrounds and abilities of pupils starting A-level courses whether at schools, sixth form centres or colleges. Many of the students will be studying a wide range of courses, which in some cases will be a mixture of science, arts and humanities.

The ABAL individualised learning materials offer a guided approach to A-level biology and can be used to form a coherent base in many teaching situations. The materials are organised so that teachers can prepare study programmes suited to their own students. The separation of core and extension work enables the academic needs of all students to be satisfied. Teachers are essential to the success of this course, not only in using their traditional skills but for organising resources and solving individual problems. They act as a personal tutors, and monitor the progress of each student as he or she proceeds through the course.

The materials aim to help the students develop and improve their personal study skills, enabling them to work more effectively and become more actively involved and responsible for their own learning and assessment. This approach allows the students to develop a sound understanding of fundamental biological concepts.

# How to use this unit

This is not a textbook. It is a guide that will help you learn as effectively as possible. As you work through it, you will be directed to practical work, audio-visual resources and other materials. There are sections of text in this guide which are to be read as any other book, but much of the guide is concerned with helping you through activities designed to produce effective learning. The following list gives details of the ways in which the unit is organised.

## (1) Objectives

Objectives are stated at the beginning of each section. They are important because they tell you what you should be able to do when you have finished working through the section. They should give you extra help in organising your learning. In particular, you should check after working through each section that you can achieve all the stated objectives and that you have notes which cover them all.

## (2) Self-assessment questions (*SAQ*)

These are designed to help you think about what you are reading. You should always write down answers to self-assessment questions and then check them immediately with those answers given at the back of this unit. If you do not understand a question and answer, make a note of it and discuss it with your tutor at the earliest opportunity.

## (3) Summary assignments

There are sixteen of these. They are designed to provide you with a set of notes. They should be carried out carefully and should be checked by your tutor for accuracy.

## (4) Self tests

There are one or more self tests for each section. They should be attempted a few days after you have completed the relevant work and not immediately after. They will help you identify what you have not understood or remembered from a particular section. You can then remedy any weaknesses identified. If you cannot answer any questions and do not understand the answers given, then check with your tutor.

## (5) Tutor assessed work

At intervals through the unit you will meet an instruction to show work to your tutor. This will enable your tutor to monitor your progress through the unit and to see how well you are coping with the material. Your tutor will then know how best to meet your individual needs.

## (6) Past examination questions

At various points in the unit you will come across past examination questions. These are only included where they are relevant to the topic under study and have been selected both to improve your knowledge of that topic and also to give you practice in answering examination questions.

## (7) Audio-visual material

A number of activities in this unit refer to video sequences which may be available from your tutor. They deal with topics which cannot be covered easily in text or practical work as well as providing a change from the normal type of learning activities. This should help motivate you.

## (8) Extension work

This work is provided for several reasons:
(*a*) to provide additional material of general interest,
(*b*) to provide more detailed treatment of some topics,
(*c*) to provide more searching questions that will make demands on your powers of thinking and reasoning.

## (9) Practicals

These are an integral part of the course and have been designed to lead you to a deeper understanding of the factual material. You will need to organise your time with care so that you can carry out the work suggested in a logical sequence. If your A-level examination requires your practical notebook to be assessed, you must be careful to keep a record of this work in a separate book.

## (10) Discussions

Whenever you attempt to learn new concepts, it is very helpful to discuss them with others at the same stage of learning. So, when a sufficient number of your class (at least three, but not more than five) have covered the material, you should have a group discussion. The idea is to get group individuals to explain the concepts in their own words and for them to be questioned by other members of the group if what they say is not clear.

## (11) Post-test

A post-test is available from you tutor when you finish this unit. This will be based on past examination questions and will give you an idea of how well you have coped with the material in this unit. It will also indicate which areas you should consolidate before going on to the next unit.

## Study and practical skills

The ABAL introductory unit *Inquiry and investigation in biology* introduced certain study and practical skills which will be practiced and improved in this unit. These include:
(*a*) the construction of graphs, histograms and tables;
(*b*) the analysis of data;
(*c*) drawing of biological specimens;
(*d*) use of the light microscope;
(*e*) the design of practical investigations.
You are also required to search for information from reference books in this unit.

## Pre-knowledge for this unit

You should have an understanding of the following:

Mammalian circulatory system
Mitotic cell division

# Introduction to this unit

Life is seen as occurring in an uninterrupted sequence from its first origins until the present day, though many changes and developments have taken place. Individual organisms come into existence, grow, develop to maturity and die. During this sequence, reproduction may occur, giving rise to the next generation which repeats the pattern. The progressive changes which an organism undergoes between its origin and its death are represented by its life-cycle. This unit studies the various parts of the life-cycle of a variety of organisms.

Individual organisms have a brief existence. Life is hazardous, especially in its early phases. Predation and hostile environmental conditions mean that the majority of organisms die before attaining their maximum possible life-span. The primary function of reproduction is to produce new individuals. This ensures that life continues and that the species will survive in spite of the death of individual organisms.

Most organisms begin their life as a single cell which grows and develops into a mature individual. For multicellular organisms this growth will involve cell division, differentiation and development. Some animal cells, e.g. blood cells and cells lining the gut have a limited life-span and need constant replacement. All the proteins in the body cells are constantly being broken down and resynthesised. As time passes, errors of replacement occur and the organism gradually accumulates defects. This process is referred to as ageing or **senescence.** Similar phenomena occur in plants. The leaves of deciduous trees show senescence each year. The whole tree also ages from the wear of damaged parts and shows a reduced growth rate. The end of the ageing process is death.

Growth and reproduction are defined as fundamental characteristics of all living organisms. Developmental changes also occur in most organisms but they may be difficult to detect in very simple organisms.

# Section 1 Growth

## 1.1 Introduction and objectives

The word growth may suggest ideas such as an increase in size and mass. A baby is carefully weighed and measured to show whether or not it is growing as it should. At the same time, other changes are occurring which cannot be detected in this way. Maturation of nerve cells, for example, makes possible an increased control over body movements and enables the baby to detect and respond to new environmental factors. A seed planted in a moist substrate increases in size and mass due to uptake of water but this is not described as growth for no new living material is formed. The seed germinates and grows into a mature plant altering considerably in size and shape. Roots, stems and leaves appear and, as the plant matures, flowers, fruits and seeds are also produced. The name development is given to these clear structural and behavioural changes which occur at the same time as an increase in size and mass.

After completing this section you should be able to do the following:
(a) Define the terms individual growth, population growth, development and differentiation.
(b) Describe how the above terms are used in relation to cells, organisms and populations.
(c) State two criteria of growth.
(d) Discuss the problems which arise in measuring growth.
(e) Measure and record growth in *Mucor hiemalis*.
(f) Calculate growth rates and discuss growth patterns from data presented in tabular and graphical form.
(g) Describe the phases in the life-cycle of a cell.
(h) Explain how mitotic cell division can lead to rapid growth of a multicellular organism.
(i) Recognise and draw cells in different stages of primary growth (division, expansion and differentiation) in a stem or root tip.
(j) Compare cell growth and the distribution of growing regions in animals and plants.
(k) State the problems which arise in following population growth in unicellular organisms.
(l) Describe the typical population growth pattern of yeast.
(m) Describe possible causes of the lag, log and plateau phases of population growth.
(n) Explain what a mathematical model is and derive one for yeast population growth.
(o) Interpret growth curves for a variety of organisms.
(p) *Extension.* (a) Define and give examples of allometric growth.
(q) List the external and internal factors affecting growth.

## 1.2 Definitions

The processes of growth and development are characteristic of all living organisms. They are very closely related processes and distinguishing between them can be difficult.

In this section you will be given definitions of the terms growth and development and also an outline of how these terms are used.

Throughout this unit, the following definitions will be used:

**Growth** — will be defined in two quite distinct ways, both of which are **quantitative.**
(a) **Individual growth** is a permanent increase in the biomass of a cell or organism. (Biomass refers to the mass of living material.)
(b) **Population growth** is an increase in the number of individuals in a population.

If a process is described simply as growth, then this will indicate that it refers to individual growth.

**Development** — is a change in the anatomy, physiology or behaviour of an organism which occurs as part of its maturation into an adult form. This term will not be used with reference to single cells of a multicellular organism.

**Differentiation** — is a change in the anatomy or physiology of a single cell or group of cells (tissue) in a multicellular organism as it matures into a specialised cell or tissue. This term is used in preference to development when referring to the cells and tissues of multicellular organisms. Both differentiation and development are **qualitative** terms.

## 1.3 Measurement of individual growth

To show that an organism or cell is growing:
(a) an increase in biomass must be demonstrated:
(b) this increase must be shown to be permanent.

The growth of an individual cell is difficult to measure. Therefore, growth measurements are generally made on whole organisms or on clearly distinguishable parts of the multicellular organisms. Either the mass of the organism is found or another dimension selected, such as the area or volume of the whole body or one of its parts. Such measurements can be obtained without damaging the organism in the course of the investigation.

1    **Mean mass of boys and girls**

| Age | Boys' mass (kg) | Girls' mass (kg) |
| --- | --- | --- |
| Birth | 3.40 | 3.36 |
| 2 years | 12.56 | 12.29 |
| 4 | 16.51 | 16.42 |
| 6 | 21.91 | 21.09 |
| 8 | 27.76 | 26.35 |
| 10 | 32.61 | 31.89 |
| 12 | 38.28 | 39.74 |
| 14 | 48.81 | 49.17 |
| 16 | 58.83 | 53.07 |
| 18 | 63.05 | 54.39 |

The figures in the table (figure 1) are the means of measurements of masses of thousands of individual boys and girls taken at two-year intervals over eighteen years.

*SAQ 1* (a) Construct a graph from the above figures to compare the pattern of growth in boys and girls. (b) Comment on any differences in the patterns shown in the graph.

The measurement of growth in this case was fairly straightforward. Because thousands of boys and girls were measured, any individual deviations between mass recorded and true biomass could be ignored.

*SAQ 2* Give an example of how a deviation between recorded mass and true biomass could occur in the above investigation.

The measurement of growth in higher plants is usually not as straightforward as in animals. Imagine that you wanted to compare the growth patterns of two types of tree over a period of twenty years.

*SAQ 3* (a) Why could you not use the same technique for trees as for human beings in the previous example? (b) Suggest two alternative methods which could be used with trees.

**Sampling** is a technique which involves collecting a number of individuals from a population. When the sample is measured, the mean value obtained is used as an estimate of the mean for the whole population. To compare the growth patterns of the trees, supposing there were two thousand of each type of tree, twenty could be cut down every two years and the mean biomass calculated.

*SAQ 4* What problems would arise in using this sampling technique?

Alternatively, if the biomass cannot be continually measured, a different characteristic may be selected. In the example used above, you could decide to measure the height of the trees.

*SAQ 5* What assumption(s) are made in using different characteristics as a measure of growth?

The results shown in the table (figure 2) were

obtained by measuring the height, number of leaves, wet mass and dry mass of a population of one hundred oat plants over a period of seventy days. The values in the table are means of the measurements from ten randomly selected plants.

### 2   Growth in oat plants

| Days from sowing | Height (cm) | No. of leaves | Wet mass (g) | Dry mass (g) |
| --- | --- | --- | --- | --- |
| 0 | — | — | 0.066 | 0.040 |
| 7 | — | — | 0.114 | 0.029 |
| 14 | 9.5 | 1 | 0.212 | 0.033 |
| 21 | 17.0 | 2 | 0.355 | 0.044 |
| 28 | 25.3 | 3 | 0.870 | 0.095 |
| 35 | 38.0 | 4 | 1.937 | 0.177 |
| 42 | 48.5 | 8 | 4.050 | 0.380 |
| 49 | 55.0 | 10 | 8.350 | 0.760 |
| 56 | 65.7 | 13 | 17.000 | 1.500 |
| 63 | 78.5 | 26 | 30.300 | 2.430 |
| 70 | 85.0 | 48 | 60.800 | 5.100 |

Rather than measuring **fresh** or **wet mass,** the plant material can be heated to drive off all water and its **dry mass** measured. Dry mass is a more reliable measure of biomass than wet mass although obviously more difficult to obtain.

*SAQ 6* (*a*) Why is dry mass a more reliable measure of biomass than wet mass?
(*b*) Construct a graph to compare the patterns of growth illustrated using the four different characteristics in figure 2.
(*c*) Comment on any differences in pattern and state, giving your reasons, whether you would regard the characteristics as reliable measures of growth.

The two examples have introduced you to several methods of measuring growth, namely by: wet mass, height, dry mass or number of leaves.

Different methods are appropriate to different organisms and circumstances. Other methods that may be used to measure growth are: volume, organ size, leaf area or internode length.

Each kind of measurement is referred to as a **criterion of growth.** A criterion (plural: criteria) is a standard of judgement. Criteria are selected on the basis of practicality and reliability.

*SAQ 7* Which two criteria would you select to measure the growth of the following?
(*a*) A baby between birth and two years.
(*b*) A crop of barley in a three-acre field over a period of three months.
(*c*) Conifers in a Forestry Commission plantation.
(*d*) Young turkeys being fattened for Christmas on two different diets. (One criterion only required.)

---

**Practical A: Measuring the growth of *Mucor hiemalis***

---

### Introduction

*Mucor hiemalis* is a species of fungus which grows on the surface of decaying bread, fruit or other organic matter. Its structure consists of a multinucleate mass of cytoplasm enclosed within a rigid, branched system of tubes, with a fairly uniform diameter, called a **mycelium.** The threads of the mycelium are called **hyphae** (singular: hypha) and fungal growth occurs only at the tip of these as they extend into and along their food source. Reproductive structures containing spores grow vertically and represent a relatively simple form of development in this organism (see figure 3).

### 3   *Mucor hiemalis,* scanning electron micograph × 150

Sporangiophore    Mycelium

Sporangium

Measuring the mass of such an organism would be very difficult because of its small size and its close relationship with its food source. In the following practical, therefore, you will measure the increase in area of the mycelium and use this as a criterion for growth.

## Materials

*Mucor hiemalis* spore suspension, Petri dish containing malt extract agar, fine felt-tip pen, sterile Pasteur pipette, sellotape, microscope, tracing paper and millimetre graph paper, sterile 10 cm$^3$ syringe

## Procedure

(*a*) Using a sterile Pasteur pipette, transfer one small drop of the suspension to the middle of the malt extract agar plate. This should be done quickly to avoid contamination. Only lift the lid of the Petri dish slightly and avoid breathing on the plates. Replace the lid as quickly as possible.
(*b*) Allow the plate to dry for ten minutes.
(*c*) Label the plate. Attach lid with sellotape.
(*d*) Turn the plate over and mark the limits of the spore drop using the felt-tip pen. Leave the plate at room temperature.
(*e*) Repeat stage (*d*) at one-day intervals to make a record of the *Mucor* growth (see figure 4) for four days.

4    **Recording growth of *Mucor***

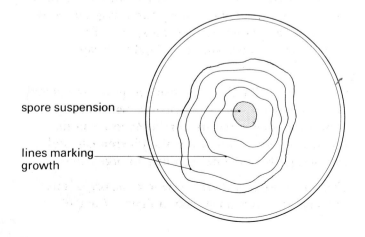

spore suspension

lines marking growth

(*f*) Use graph paper to calculate each day's increase in area. Trace the growth areas from the dish onto the graph paper. Count each complete millimetre square. Ignore squares *less* than half included. Count as one square all squares more than half included.

## Discussion of Results

1 Collect mean class results and construct a graph to show the pattern of growth of *Mucor hiemalis.*
2 Write a careful discussion of your results. Suggest possible reasons for the variations in growth observed. (Section 1.10 may help you with this.)

Show this work to your tutor.

## 1.4 Summary assignment 1

1 Define the terms: individual growth, population growth, development and differentiation.
2 Construct a table (see figure 5) including all the criteria for growth mentioned in this section.

Show this work to your tutor.

5    **Table for summary assignment 1**

| Criterion | Advantages | Disadvantages | Suitable for e.g. |
|---|---|---|---|
| e.g. height or length of whole organism | | | |

## 1.5 Growth and the cell cycle

A cell grows by assimilating materials from its environment. **Assimilation** involves not only absorbing these materials across its cell membrane but also incorporating them into its biomass. As a cell grows, it will be either preparing to divide into daughter cells or developing into a mature form with a particular structure or function. A cycle of events can be drawn up for the life of the cell in a similar way to that for whole organisms. In this section, only **somatic** cells are being considered. These are all the cells of a living organism apart from the reproductive cells. Somatic cells undergo a form of nuclear division called **mitosis** but some reproductive cells also go through a nuclear division process called **meiosis.** (Meiosis will be studied in section 3 of this unit.)

The life-cycle of a somatic cell from the time of its formation until the time it divides into two daughter cells may be divided into five phases. These are summarised below.

**Cytokinesis (C):** this is the phase in which cell division by the splitting of the cytoplasm occurs. The splitting is controlled so that the two nuclei formed during mitosis (nuclear division) in the previous phase are separated, one into each daughter cell.

**Pre-synthetic phase (G1):** after cytokinesis, the new daughter cells undergo a period of reorganisation in which their organelles are arranged in preparation for the synthetic phase. During this phase there is some synthesis of materials needed in the next phase.

**Synthetic phase (S):** in this phase chromatin, which is composed of DNA and protein, is synthesised. This results in a doubling of chromosome number as each DNA molecule is faithfully copied.

**Post-synthetic phase (G2):** this involves the preparation of the spindle apparatus which is used to separate the paired chromosomes in the following mitotic phase.

**Mitosis (M):** paired chromosomes are separated and sorted into two identical sets and the nucleus divides. After this, cytokinesis occurs and the life-cycle of the somatic cell is completed.

The complete cell cycle which includes mitosis is often referred to as mitotic cell division or, simply, mitosis. Mitosis, however, occupies only a small portion of the cell cycle and the use of such terms for the whole cycle is incorrect. The pre-synthetic, synthetic and post-synthetic phases are often referred to collectively as **interphase.**

Figure 6 illustrates this sequence of events and the length of arc given to each phase corresponds to the relative time taken, on average, for that phase to occur.

## 6   The cell cycle

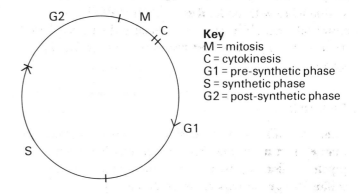

Key
M = mitosis
C = cytokinesis
G1 = pre-synthetic phase
S = synthetic phase
G2 = post-synthetic phase

The details of mitosis are covered in the unit *Cells and the origin of life.*

Self test 1, page 107, covers mitosis. If you find difficulty in completing it, you should spend some time revising this topic.

It would also be useful to view the videotape showing mitosis in the endosperm of *Haemanthus katherinae* at this stage. See AV6, *Cells and the origin of life.*

Cell division occurs in two steps: mitosis, the division of the nucleus into two identical nuclei and cytokinesis, the division of the cell containing two nuclei into two cells each containing a nucleus. Cell division in unicellular organisms results in two separate individuals and thus population growth occurs (see section 1.2). In multicellular organisms, the cells remain attached and the growth of the new cells contributes to the growth of the whole organism. The fertilised egg which gives rise to an adult human being is the first of about thirty-two cell generations (divisions) and as growth proceeds, the cells differentiate and become specialised to perform different functions.

In summary, all cells and organisms grow (individual growth) by increasing their biomass permanently; population growth results from an increase in the number of individuals. Cells also differentiate and this brings about the development of organisms.

The relationship of these terms to cells, organisms and populations is illustrated in figures 7 and 8.

## 7 Growth and development in single-celled organisms

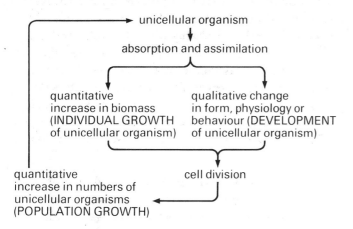

## 8 Growth, development and differentiation in multicellular organisms

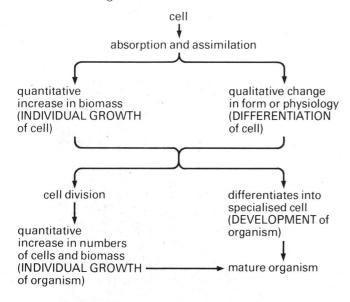

## 1.6 Growth in mammals

Cell division in mammals makes a very important contribution to overall growth but cell division is not always followed by an increase in cell size.

Cell division during the earliest stages of embryonic development (see section 9) leads to an increase in cell numbers without change in volume or mass. The cells of some animal tissues undergo constant cell divisions and other tissues are able to begin division when necessary. There are, however, certain animal tissues that are not capable of cell division once they have differentiated. Figure 9 gives examples of the three types of tissues.

## 9 Cell division in tissues

| Actively dividing tissues | Tissues able to divide when neccessary | Tissues unable to divide |
|---|---|---|
| Epidermis | Liver | Voluntary muscle |
| Epithelia | Kidney | Neurons |
| Blood-forming tissues (*not* red blood cells) | Connective tissues | Germ cells of the ovary |
| Uterus lining | Exocrine glands | |
| Germ cells of the testis | Skeletal tissues (in part) | |

There are limits to the growth and size of mammals as indeed of most animals. Mammals have a definite size and shape, a fact which is closely connected with the need to be able to move freely. Some mammals, when provided with an unlimited food supply, may increase in girth after normal growth has ceased. This is, however, due to the deposition of fat in adipose tissue and is not due to permanent increase in biomass or cell number. Growth of bones in animals depends much on the secretion of inorganic and organic materials by bone cells but these deposits are permanent.

## 1.7 Growth in flowering plants

Division of the cells of flowering plants after the very earliest stages of life is restricted to regions called **meristems.** There are two general types of meristem and they give rise to two different kinds of growth. Primary growth largely contributes to an increase in the length of the plants and originates in **apical meristems** at the tips of stems and roots. Secondary growth contributes to an increase in girth and originates in the **lateral meristems** which occur away from the tips, near the periphery of the root and stem. Figure 10 illustrates the position of these sites in the stem and root tips.

## 10  Plant meristems

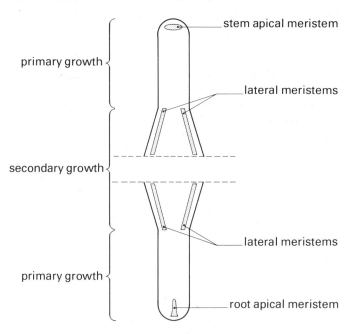

Cytokinesis in plant cells occurs by the formation of a **cell plate,** a thin layer of polysaccharide material surrounded by membranes. It is formed by the fusion of vesicles, probably from the Golgi body, which accumulate across the spindle between the two daughter nuclei as mitosis is completed. This cell plate grows outwards until it reaches the cell wall. Cellulose is deposited on each side and the cell plate becomes the **middle lamella** which separates the two cells. This process can be seen in some cells of figure 11.

Both daughter cells will grow by assimilation of nutrients. If they are to remain **meristematic** (dividing) cells, they will then divide again, otherwise they begin to elongate due to uptake of water and development of vacuoles. Finally, these cells will differentiate into their permanent form. Figure 12 shows the changes a plant cell may go through during growth.

## 11  Cytokinesis in root tip of *Allium*

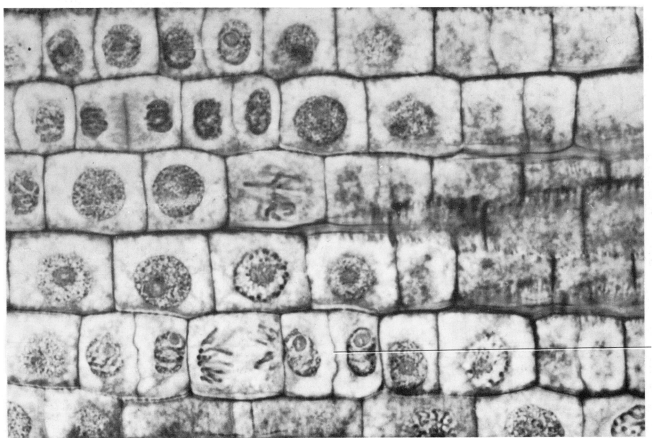

## 12  The changes in a plant cell during growth

### The stages of primary growth

| Stage 1: Growth by division | Stage 2: Growth by cell expansion | Stage 3: Differentiation Development |

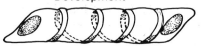

Cells in the meristematic region divide producing an increase in the number

Small vacuoles become visible and enlarge by water uptake. As they enlarge they coalesce to produce one large central vacuole. The cell wall is stretched but some new material is also deposited

The cells differentiate into their permanent form. This usually involves the formation of a characteristic cell wall in addition to internal changes. A spirally thickened wall of a type of xylem cell is illustrated

Cell growth or permanent increase in biomass occurs in the regions of cell division and cell expansion. Thus, increase in length of stems and roots occurs only towards the apex of the stem and root. Growth in roots is illustrated by the photographs in figure 13.

Trees and shrubs, unlike animals, are not limited in their growth. However, they tend to grow to a shape characteristic of their species. Trees continue to increase in height and girth but growth rates slow with increased age. The biomass of trees can far exceed that of the largest known animal — the blue whale. The giant redwood may reach a mass of one million kg whereas a blue whale only reaches a mass of about 120 000 kg.

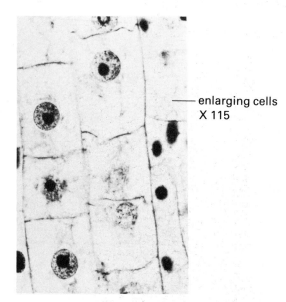

— enlarging cells
X 115

### 13  Root tip of broad bean showing regions of division, elongation and differentiation

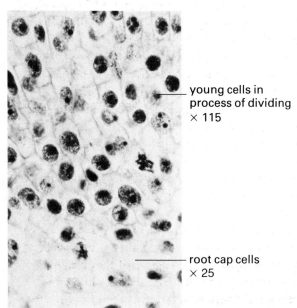

— young cells in process of dividing
× 115

— root cap cells
× 25

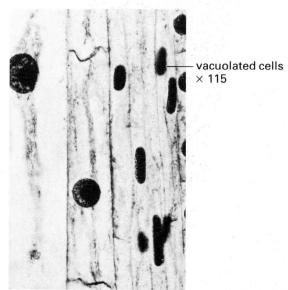

— vacuolated cells
× 115

*SAQ 8* Construct a table to show three differences between growth in mammals and flowering plants.

## Practical B: Observing regions of primary growth in the root tip of *Vicia faba* (broad bean)

### Introduction

This practical involves microscopic examination of a squashed root tip of *Vicia faba* in which the three stages of primary growth should be evident. Two of these stages are shown in figure 14.

**14   LS of the root tip of *Vicia faba***

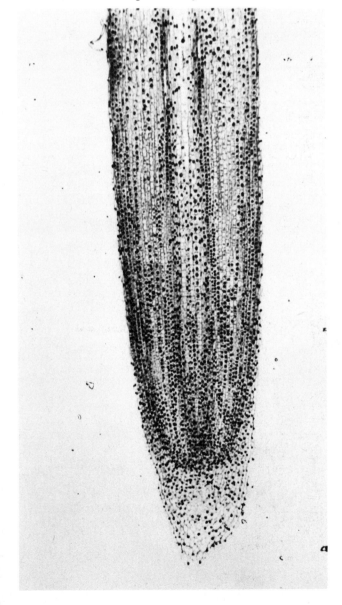

In addition to observing the primary growth stages, you may also be able to observe cells undergoing mitotic division in the meristematic region. A chromosome stain, acetic-orcein, is therefore used in the procedure.

### Materials

germinating broad bean with growing root, ☠ 25 cm³ 1 M hydrochloric acid (liquid corrosive, liquid and vapour poisonous), 5 cm³ acetic-orcein, water-bath (60 °C) and thermometer, microscope and lamp, prepared slide (LS of root tip), 4 glass slides and coverslips, 4 specimen tubes, razor blade, forceps, mounted needle, filter paper, glass rod, 5 cm³ syringe

### Procedure

(*a*) Label four slides A, B, C and D.
(*b*) Select a bean with a healthy root. This will have a yellow and white pointed tip which has grown well away from the root-hair region. Place the root on a slide and cut off 10 mm from the root tip.
(*c*) Cut up the 10 mm section into four equal sections.
(*d*) Transfer each section to a labelled slide noting which slide contains which section.
(*e*) Keep the sections moist with water.
(*f*) Use a syringe to place 5 cm³ of 1 M hydrochloric acid in each of four specimen tubes. TAKE CARE!
(*g*) Label the tubes A, B, C and D.
(*h*) Heat the tubes to 60 °C in a water-bath.
(*i*) Transfer the sections individually to the appropriately-labelled tube, using a mounted needle.
(*j*) Leave for ten minutes whilst the combination of acid and heat softens the tissue.
(*k*) Remove each section back to the appropriate slide and wash it.
(*l*) Use a glass rod to add a drop of acetic-orcein to each section. This will stain the chromosome material.
(*m*) Break each section up with the mounted needle.
(*n*) Cover each section with a coverslip and gently tap the coverslip with the handle of the mounted needle to spread the cells. Squash the slide and coverslip gently between sheets of filter paper. (Avoid

any sideways pressure on the coverslip — this tends to roll up the flattened cells.)

(*o*) Examine the slides with a microscope.

(*p*) Draw and label cells which are typical of those in the regions of division, enlargement and differentiation.

(*q*) If you have carried out the procedure particularly well, you may be able to see various stages of mitoses in the cell division region. Draw and label these mitotic cells.

(*r*) Examine the prepared slide of a root tip and trace a line of cells from the meristematic region backwards. Note and draw any changes in the cells as you work backwards.

Show this work to your tutor.

## 1.8 Population growth of unicellular organisms

Population growth of unicellular organisms is a consequence of cell division. The criterion for population growth is an increase in the number of individuals in a population.

In order to follow population growth, it is necessary to count accurately the number of individuals in a population at specified time intervals. Unicellular organisms are small, usually microscopic, and this section examines the practical techniques for dealing with the problems which arise in counting microscopic organisms, using yeast as an example.

The yeasts are single-celled organisms with considerable economic importance. They are adapted to living in environments with a high sugar content and many of them (fermentative yeasts) have the ability to ferment sugars forming ethanol and carbon dioxide. This ability has been exploited for thousands of years in the production of beer, wine and bread.

Yeasts are typically ovoid and multiply by forming buds (**budding**). The buds enlarge until they are almost equal in size to the parent cell. Nuclear division occurs and then a cross-wall is formed between the two cells. Eventually, they may separate. The photomicrograph (figure 15) was taken

**15 Budding yeast (*Saccharomyces cerevisiae*)**

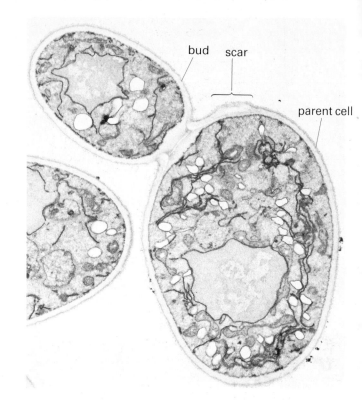

with an electron microscope. It shows a bud forming from a parent cell which also bears the scar left from a previous bud to the right of the new bud.

Following the growth of a population of yeast over a period of time presents certain difficulties. The individual cell is very small and a microscope must be used to observe it. It may be difficult to discriminate between yeast cells and contaminating organisms. It may be difficult to decide between living and dead cells. It is often difficult to decide if two yeast cells close together are a mother cell with a bud or two separate cells.

*Schizosaccharomyces pombe* is a species of yeast having certain characteristics which make it useful in studying yeast growth. It is relatively large (16 $\mu$m long and 3.5 $\mu$m wide) and it grows by increasing its length whilst maintaining a cylindrical shape. Also, it reproduces by **binary fission,** splitting transversely into two when its maximum size is attained. The life-cycle of *Schizosaccharomyces pombe* is illustrated in figure 16.

## 16   The life-cycle of *S. pombe*

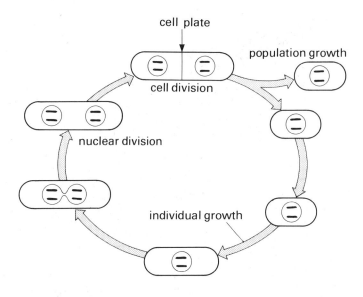

cell plate

population growth

cell division

nuclear division

individual growth

**SAQ 9** (*a*) State two advantages *S. pombe* has over most budding yeasts for biologists studying yeast growth.
(*b*) Why is it important to study other species of yeast as well as *S. pombe* before making general statements about yeasts?

---

## Practical C: Using a haemocytometer

---

### Introduction

The haemocytometer is a piece of apparatus used to estimate the number of cells or microorganisms in a given volume of culture. In this section, it will be used to follow the population growth of yeast. The haemocytometer is more commonly used in medical practice to count the number of blood cells in a sample of blood.

The apparatus consists of a thick glass slide with channels cut across it, which are on either side of a lowered central platform (see figure 17).

When the cover-glass is in position, a chamber of known depth (0.1 mm) is created. The central area of the platform has a number of lines etched on it. These are shown in figure 18.

The design of the haemocytometer insures that when the coverslip is in position a film of cell suspension of standard volume will always be formed over each square. By counting the cells within a typical square, the density of the suspension from which a sample has been taken may be calculated.

### Materials

haemocytometer slide and coverslip (specially thickened), tissue paper, Pasteur pipette or syringe and needle, culture of yeast cells, microscope

### Procedure

(*a*) Clean the haemocytometer slide and coverslip with a dry tissue.
(*b*) Breathe on the slide to moisten it slightly and then slide the coverslip slowly on to the slide, as shown in figure 19.
(*c*) The index figures should exert a downward pressure where the coverslip is in contact with the slide as the coverslip is pushed along by the thumbs.
(*d*) A rainbow effect (Newton's rings) should be seen where the coverslip and slide are in contact, if viewed from a shallow angle.

## 17   A haemocytometer

(*a*) **Top view**

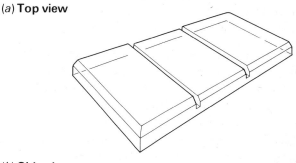

(*b*) **Side view**

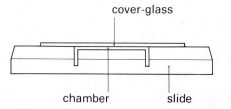

cover-glass

chamber          slide

## 18 The line markings on a haemocytometer slide

### (a) Total marked area

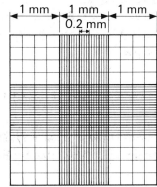

The total area marked out is 9 mm². The central square which you will be using is 1 mm² and has 25 smaller squares within it (each 0.04 mm²)

### (b) Central marked area

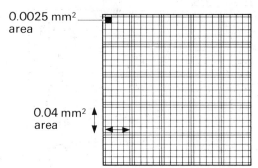

These have triple lines delineating them and 16 even smaller squares within them (each 0.0025 mm²)

## 19 Fitting a coverslip

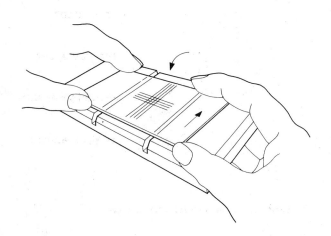

(*e*) One edge of the coverslip should project very slightly beyond the outer, vertical edge of the slide.
(*f*) Now take a sterile Pasteur pipette (or syringe and needle). Shake the culture to disperse the cells evenly. Use the pipette to transfer a drop of the suspension to the slide, as shown in figure 20.
(*g*) The space between the platform and the slip should be almost completely filled. However, there should not be any suspension in the channels around the platform.
(*h*) If air bubbles become trapped under the coverslip, or if the channels get any liquid in them, clean the slide and start again.

(*i*) Put the slide on the microscope stage and allow one minute for the cells to settle.
(*j*) Focus the low-power ( × 10) and then the high-power ( × 40) objective lens on the central area of the counting chamber.
(*k*) Count the cells in four 0.04 mm² areas of the twenty-five squares in the central area.
(*l*) Some cells will lie on or touch a line between areas. It is usual to count any cells which touch the north or west boundaries of an area (even if they are mostly in the neighbouring area) and ignore any which touch the south or east boundaries. This is illustrated in figure 21, where in the square marked

## 20 Introducing a drop of culture under the coverslip

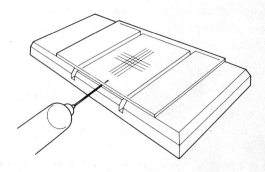

## 21  Cells in a haemocytometer

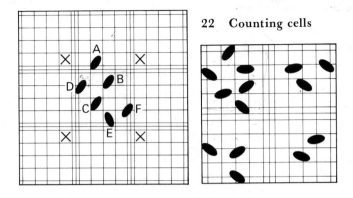

### 22  Counting cells

by Xs, the cells labelled A, B, C and D would be counted as being in that square but the cells labelled E and F would not.

### Discussion of results

1 Calculate the mean number of cells for the four areas counted.
2 Calculate from this mean number an estimate of the number of cells per cm$^3$ in the original culture. Remember that the area counted was 0.04 mm$^2$ and the depth of liquid was 0.1 mm.
3 Check your calculation for (2) above by comparing it with the worked example which follows.

Show this work to your tutor.

*Calculation method for working out culture density.*

1 Four squares are shown in figure 22 with cells indicated by black dots.
2 The counts are 3, 5, 2, 2.
3 The mean count is $\dfrac{3 + 5 + 2 + 2}{4} = 3$.
4 Three cells, on average are found in a 0.04 mm$^2$ area and 1 mm$^2$ = 0.04 mm$^2$ × 25
∴ in a 1 mm$^2$ area one would expect 3 × 25 cells = 75.
5 Seventy-five cells are estimated in 1 mm$^2$ area of 0.1 mm depth = 0.1 mm$^3$ volume.
1 cm$^3$ = 0.1 mm$^3$ × 10$^4$

∴ in a volume of 1 cm$^3$ one would expect 75 × 10$^4$ cells = 7.5 × 10$^5$.
The answer therefore is 7.5 × 10$^5$ cells.
The simple rule is to multiply your average calculation for a 0.04 mm$^2$ area by 25 × 10$^4$ to work out the number per cm$^3$.

### 1.8.1 A mathematical model for yeast population growth

Figure 23 represents how a yeast population would grow from a single cell if reproducing by binary fission.

If the time taken for each yeast cell to grow and split into two is $t$ seconds, then it is possible to construct a graph (see figure 24) which represents the expected

### 23  Yeast population growth

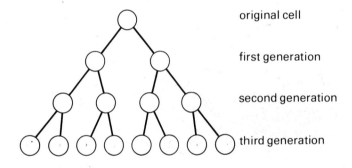

### 24  A graph of yeast population growth

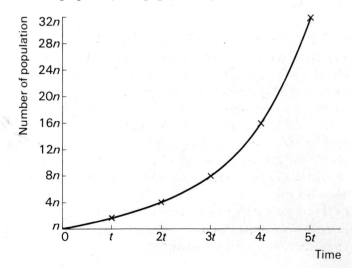

15

pattern of population growth starting with any number (represented by $n$ in the graph).

This graph is a mathematical model of yeast population growth. It could be represented even more concisely by the mathematical formula for the curve ($y = \dfrac{2^x}{2}$ where $x$ is the generation number).

Mathematical models are very useful in biology for a number of reasons. One of these is that they enable predictions to be made which can be tested by experiment . If the prediction is not confirmed by experiment, then the model must be modified in some way to fit the observations more precisely.

*SAQ 10* The mathematical model for yeast population growth is based on two assumptions. What are these?

From this model, it can be predicted that for a population of yeast, monitored over a period of time, the growth pattern will resemble that shown in the graph (figure 24). This prediction can be tested by examining the results obtained from an actual investigation into population growth in a culture of *Schizosaccharomyces pombe*.

A culture of *S. pombe* was placed in a water-bath at 32 °C (the optimum temperature for growth in this species). Samples were removed from the culture by means of a Pasteur pipette at 15-minute intervals over a span of three hours. The cell number was calculated. The results are given in figure 25.

**25   The results of an investigation into population growth of yeast over a period of three hours**

| Time (hrs) | Cell No. $\times 10^6$ |
| --- | --- |
| 0.00 | 2.14 |
| 0.25 | 2.17 |
| 0.50 | 2.06 |
| 0.75 | 2.05 |
| 1.00 | 2.11 |
| 1.25 | 2.26 |
| 1.50 | 2.09 |
| 1.75 | 2.26 |
| 2.00 | 2.53 |
| 2.25 | 3.15 |
| 2.50 | 3.85 |
| 2.75 | 3.88 |
| 3.00 | 3.89 |

*SAQ 11* Construct a graph showing population growth in yeast from the information provided.

*SAQ 12* Compare this graph with the model graph given in figure 24. Write down points of difference and points of similarity between the two graphs.

*SAQ13* Suggest possible reasons for the results obtained in the last half hour of the investigations.

### 1.8.2 Curves representing population growth

Figure 26 shows a generalised curve for population growth of cells such as yeasts, unicellular green algae or bacteria when plotted against time. Such a curve is described as being S-shaped or **sigmoid.**

**26   Growth of a population of cells**

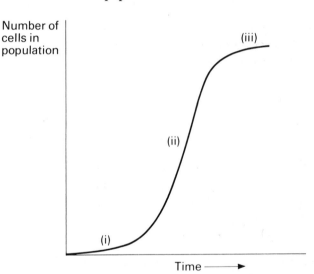

Three main phases can be distinguished in such a curve and can be related to growing populations under **limiting conditions.** (A population growing in a culture flask with non-renewable nutrients and a finite space, is growing under limiting conditions.) The phases are (i) lag phase, (ii) log phase or exponential phase, and (iii) plateau phase.

In the *lag phase (i),* population growth is slow. This may be due to cells that were previously dormant or growing slowly in an old culture requiring time to establish themselves in a new culture with a fresh supply of nutrients. *The log or exponential phase (ii)* has been explained by means of the mathematical model in section 1.8.1. This is the period of maximum population growth when all conditions are optimal. As nutrients become scarcer, space limited or, possibly, toxic waste products accumulate, then the reproductive rate falls and the curve flattens out into the *plateau phase (iii)*. Alternatively, the reproductive rate may continue unchanged but the death rate rises.

## 1.9 Growth curves for multicellular organisms

In section 1.3, you were asked to draw growth curves for boys and girls between birth and eighteen years and for oat plants from time of sowing up to seventy days' growth.

Examine these curves again. See answer to SAQ 1.

*SAQ 14* What would you except to happen to the curve for human growth if measurements had been extended for a further ten years? Give an explanation for your answer.

*SAQ 15* Predict what would happen to the growth curve for oats if the period of measurement was doubled. Again, explain your answer.

*SAQ 16* What term could be used to describe growth curves for mammals and flowering plants if the two organisms discussed above are indeed typical examples? Do you consider it likely from your own knowledge that the examples are typical?

Annual plants, the leaves of dicotyledons and stem internodes generally reach a maximum size and increase no further. Perennial woody plants have no definite maximum size and each year add more growth. Figure 27 shows the kind of growth curve which results.

*SAQ 17* Explain the shape of the growth curve in figure 27 by relating it to the seasons of the year in a temperate climate such as that of Britain.

The growth curve for most land animals is similar to that for annual plants like oats. The exact shape of the growth curve of a mammal depends upon the

### 27 Growth in a perennial woody plant

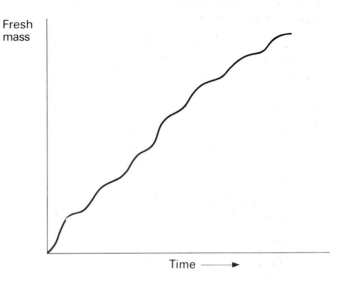

time taken to reach sexual maturity. A growth curve for the laboratory rat is a continuous sigmoid shape, whereas the growth curve for human beings, which you have already studied, shows variation in the rate of growth during infancy and puberty.

### 1.9.1 *Extension:* Allometric growth

You have seen that there are problems in deciding which characteristic to measure when investigating growth. It may have occurred to you that one common feature of the characteristics so far considered is that they are all being used to give a picture of the overall growth of an organism. However, different parts of an organism grow at

### 28 General growth curve of human body

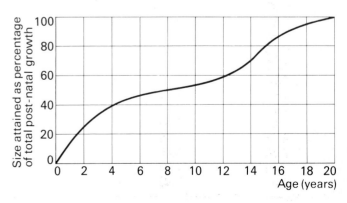

**29**  **Growth curves for the human brain and head, lymphoid tissue (thymus, lymph nodes and masses) and reproductive organs**

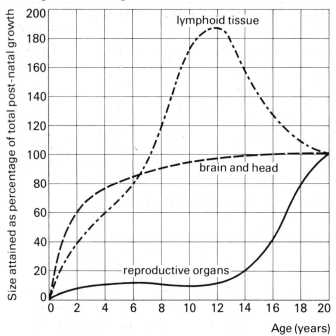

different rates — this is known as **allometric growth** and is illustrated in figures 28 and 29.

***SAQ 18*** (*a*) Compare and contrast the growth curves for (i) reproductive organs, (ii) brain and head, and (iii) lymphoid tissue, with general growth curve. (*b*) State any possible advantages to the human organism in having the particular pattern of growth illustrated for each of the different tissues.

## 1.10 Factors affecting growth

Growth is affected by a variety of factors in the external and internal environments of an organism.

A list of external factors is provided below. Your own biological knowledge should enable you to understand how these factors influence growth. Ask you tutor if you have difficulty.

— Nutrient supply, particularly of vitamins, minerals and trace elements.

— Temperature — (little effect on birds and mammals because they can regulate their internal temperature).

— Light — chiefly on plants. The effects of light on plants (other than photosynthesis) are covered in the unit *Response to the environment*. This unit also discusses the control of growth by hormones and the roles of plant hormones.

— Water supply (or humidity).

— Hydrogen ion concentration (pH).

— Accumulation of by-products of metabolism. This applies mainly to organisms living in closed environments, e.g. yeast ceases growth as the concentration of alcohol approaches fifteen per cent.

— Genetic constitution and hormones. The growth pattern of living organisms is basically controlled by their **genetic constitution.** Part of this control is brought about through the action of **hormones,** substances which act as chemical messengers. Plant and animal hormones share the characteristic of being produced in one part of the organism and having their effect on special **target cells or organs** which may be some distance away. Hormone action is particularly concerned with metabolic activities in the cytoplasm. By altering the balance of these, hormones are able to coordinate long-term changes such as growth and maturation. Animal hormones are secreted directly into the blood by **endocrine glands.**

The chief hormone involved with growth in mammals is secreted by the pituitary gland and is known as growth hormone (GH). Other hormones also influence growth. The plant hormones which have the greatest influence on the growth of flowering plants are auxins, gibberellins, cytokinins and abscissic acid.

## 1.11 Rates of growth

The sigmoid curve showing growth of populations and organisms can be related to actual rates of growth. In early stages of growth, the growth rate may be nearly exponential, but gradually, the growth rate diminishes and will approach zero growth as is shown in figure 30 which relates the growth curve for an organism to its growth rate curve.

**30** Growth and growth rate of an organism

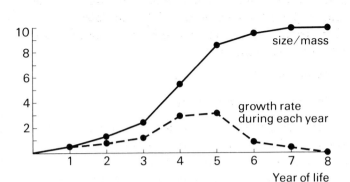

**31** Growth of lambs

| Age (wks) | Mass (kg) | | | |
|---|---|---|---|---|
| | Singles | Twins | Triplets | Twins reared as singles |
| 2 | 10.0 | 7.2 | 6.5 | 7.9 |
| 6 | 19.5 | 13.7 | 13.1 | 16.8 |
| 10 | 28.5 | 20.9 | 20.2 | 25.0 |
| 14 | 37.0 | 28.6 | 27.0 | 33.6 |
| 18 | 43.7 | 35.1 | 33.1 | 41.0 |
| 22 | 48.5 | 40.0 | 37.9 | 46.1 |
| 26 | 51.8 | 44.3 | 42.4 | 49.3 |

The following exercise is a past question from the Cambridge Local Examinations Board. Work through it carefully.

The female sheep, the ewe, may have one, two or three lambs per pregnancy. At first, the lambs feed only on milk, but after about five weeks they begin to eat solid food.

A research worker was interested in the effect of the number of lambs per ewe on the growth of lambs. To investigate this problem, he weighed lambs of different classes every four weeks. The classes were as follows:

Singles (single lambs reared by their own mother). Twins (twins reared by their own mother). Triplets (triplets reared by their own mother). Twins reared as singles (lambs born as twins, but shortly after birth one was transferred to another ewe and both lambs were reared as singles).

His data are summarised in figure 31 where each observation is the mean for a large number of lambs.
(*a*) For each period of four weeks, calculate the growth rate (as kg per four-week period) for each class and tabulate your results.
(*b*) Present your calculated data in the form of a graph of growth rate against age of lamb.
(*c*) Comment upon the differences in growth rate of the different classes.
(*d*) Do you consider that food supply is the only factor which affects the growth rate of the different classes?

Show this work to your tutor.

## 1.12 Summary assignment 2

1 Draw a large diagram to show the cell cycle and annotate it fully to include a brief explanation of each phase.
2 Draw up a table to compare growth in mammals and flowering plants. (Include points of difference and points of similarity.) Your table should include mention of: methods of growth, growth regions, growth limits, factors affecting growth.
3 Draw a typical sigmoid curve (similar to figure 25).

Indicate on the curve the following parts: lag phase, log phase, plateau phase.

For each of the following organisms, briefly explain what is happening at each of the labelled phases.
(*a*) Bacteria in a broth culture.
(*b*) A pea plant (an annual).
(*c*) A cat.

Show this work to your tutor.

Self test 2, page 107, covers section 1 of this unit.

## 1.13 *Extension:* Growth and development in mice

---

**Practical D: Growth and development in mice**

---

**Introduction**

This extension practical concerns both growth and

development of post-natal mice. Although development in animals will not be dealt with until later in this unit, it is introduced as a practical activity in this early section because of the time taken to complete the practical.

### Materials

A litter of young unweaned mice, weighing machine, ruler, 'Handling small mammals' — information sheet, reference book: *Small Mammals* by J.D. Wray (published by Hodder & Stoughton)

### Procedure

The following observations and measurements should be made and recorded at weekly intervals (for six weeks) starting between seven and twelve days after birth.
(i) Observations of changes in the external form of the mice including eyes, ears, shape of skull and snout, pigmentation, hair, activity and behaviour, sex organs.
(ii) Measurement of mass, body length and tail length.
NB Remember that young mice must be kept warm and not isolated from their mother for too long.

### Discussion of results

1 Construct a graph which compares the pattern of growth revealed by the different characteristics measured.
2 Note at the relevant points on this graph the major developmental changes which occurred.
3 Comment on any changes in the rates of growth revealed over the six-week period of observation.

Show this work to your tutor.

## 1.14 *Extension:* Cancer

In this section you have studied the process of growth and seen that in most animals there are controls over growth. When a certain size is reached, control mechanisms stop rapid cell division.

Under certain conditions, however, growth control factors cease to operate and tissues continue to grow unchecked. This uncontrolled growth of tissues beyond their normal size or cell number is called cancer.

AV 1 studies some aspects of this topic.

---

### AV 1 Cancer

---

### Materials

VCR and monitor
ABAL video sequence — *Cancer*
Worksheets

### Procedure

(*a*) Check that you have all the relevant materials for this activity.
(*b*) Check that the video cassette is set up ready to show the appropriate sequence, *Cancer*
(*c*) Start the VCR and stop it to complete the worksheets as indicated in the film.
(*d*) If you do not understand anything, stop the video, rewind, and study the relevant material again before consulting your tutor.
(*e*) If possible, work through the video and worksheets with a small group and discuss the material with your fellow students.

---

# Section 2  Asexual reproduction

## 2.1 Introduction and objectives

Reproduction is another of the *characteristics of living organisms*. Unlike other characteristics, reproduction is not essential to the survival of an individual organism, but it is important for the survival of the species to which an individual organism belongs.

By means of reproduction, new members of a species are produced. This is essential if the species is to survive, for these new individuals can replace those that have died and also allow the numbers of the species to increase.

Reproduction may be either **asexual** or **sexual.**

In *asexual* reproduction, *one parent* is involved in the production of offspring. These offspring normally arise by means of mitotic cell division and are thus usually *genetically identical* to each other and to the parent. They are known as **clones**.

In *sexual* reproduction, generally *two parents* are involved in the production of offspring. The offspring arise from the *union* of the parents' sex cells, or **gametes.** They differ from their parents and each other.

Each type of reproduction has important advantages. Asexual reproduction can lead to a rapid increase in numbers, whereas sexual reproduction leads to genetic variation within the species in addition to increasing numbers.

Asexual reproduction is directly related to growth. Mitotic cell division results in an increase in cell numbers in the growth of multicellular organisms. In unicellular organisms, it brings about an increase in the number of individuals and this is population growth.

Asexual reproduction is not limited to unicellular organisms but occurs in most groups of the plant kingdom and in those animals with relatively simple levels of body organisation. Growth occurs in

favourable conditions of good food supply, suitable temperatures and adequate space. The same conditions are associated with asexual reproduction.

The new individuals produced under favourable conditions, being genetically identical to the parent organism, are well fitted to exploit their environment and grow rapidly, thus increasing the total biomass of the species.

This section studies the actual methods of asexual reproduction used by a variety of organisms and assesses the importance of this stage in the life-cycle of organisms. Methods of asexual reproduction in plants have applications in agriculture and horticulture that are of economic importance and these too will be considered.

After working through this section, you should be able to do the following:
(*a*) Define asexual and sexual reproduction.
(*b*) State the differences between asexual and sexual reproduction.
(*c*) List the methods of asexual reproduction occurring in lower organisms.
(*d*) Give an account of asexual reproduction in protistans such as *Amoeba* or *Paramecium* and in *Hydra* and *Spirogyra*.
(*e*) Identify the organs of asexual reproduction in flowering plants and understand their functions.
(*f*) Explain the importance of asexual reproduction for all the species studied.
(*g*) List and briefly describe the methods of asexual reproduction used in agriculture and horticulture and assess their economic importance.

## 2.2 Methods of asexual reproduction in lower organisms

Section 1.8 examined population growth in yeasts and gave an account of two methods of asexual reproduction which occur in this group of unicellular fungi, namely budding and binary fission.

**SAQ 19** Re-read the account of these two processes and write down one element that is common to both budding and binary fission and three ways in which these methods of division differ.

Binary fission occurs commonly among unicellular organisms such as Protista and bacteria.

Figure 32 illustrates the process in Protista. Study it and answer the following questions.

**SAQ 20** Why is asexual reproduction described as binary fission in *Amoeba* but as transverse binary fission in *Paramecium* and longitudinal binary fission in *Euglena?*

**SAQ 21** In what major way does binary fission differ in *Paramecium* when compared with *Amoeba* and *Euglena?*

**SAQ 22** How is binary fission more complex in *Paramecium* and *Euglena* than in *Amoeba?*

The coelenterates such as *Hydra* and *Obelia* show asexual reproduction by budding. *Hydra* possesses several kinds of cell. These are shown in figure 33.

**SAQ 23** Which kind of cell is most likely to undergo mitosis leading to growth or asexual reproduction? Give reasons for your answer.

**SAQ 24** Explain how a bud could arise from mitotic division.

**SAQ 25** Is it likely that production of buds could be limited to one special region of the animal? Give a reason for your answer.

**SAQ 26** How does the production of buds in *Hydra* differ from the process in yeast?

The two other common methods of asexual reproduction in lower organisms are:

**Sporulation** — the production of microscopic **spores** which are generally specialised cells containing nucleus and cytoplasm, usually surrounded by a resistant wall able to withstand dry conditions and extremes of temperature.

Organisms producing spores include the bacteria, algae, fungi, mosses and liverworts and ferns.

**Fragmentation** — this occurs when an organism breaks into two or more pieces, each of which grows into a new individual. Organisms using this method include *Spirogyra,* and other filamentous algae, also sea anemones and starfish. This process is similar to **regeneration** when parts of an organism can rebuild tissues to form a new individual. Regeneration is seen in *Hydra*, flatworms, starfish, some annelid worms and also amphibians to some extent.

## 2.3 Summary assignment 3

Make brief notes to cover objectives (a)–(d) of this section.

Show this work to your tutor.

**32    Binary fission in *Amoeba, Paramecium* and *Euglena***

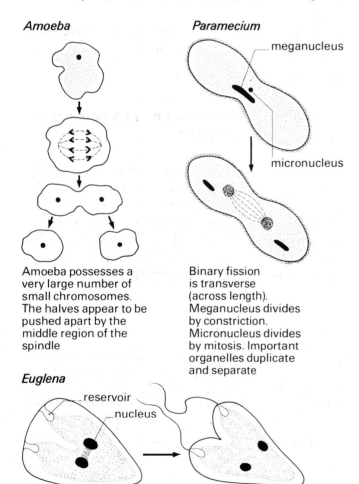

**Amoeba**

Amoeba possesses a very large number of small chromosomes. The halves appear to be pushed apart by the middle region of the spindle

**Paramecium**

meganucleus

micronucleus

Binary fission is transverse (across length). Meganucleus divides by constriction. Micronucleus divides by mitosis. Important organelles duplicate and separate

**Euglena**

reservoir
nucleus

Binary fission is longitudinal and proceeds from the anterior. Flagella bases and reservoirs duplicate before separation

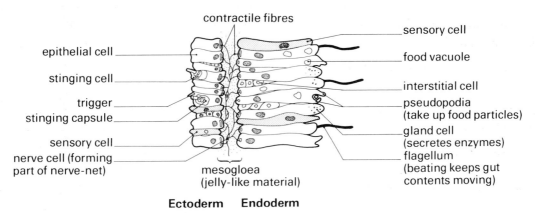

contractile fibres

sensory cell

epithelial cell

food vacuole

stinging cell

interstitial cell

trigger

pseudopodia
(take up food particles)

stinging capsule

gland cell
(secretes enzymes)

sensory cell

nerve cell (forming
part of nerve-net)

mesogloea
(jelly-like material)

flagellum
(beating keeps gut
contents moving)

**Ectoderm**    **Endoderm**

## Practical E: Asexual reproduction in lower organisms

This practical also serves as a summary exercise for this topic and involves researching information in addition to practical skills.

### Materials

specimens A–G, microscope, hand lens, information sources (e.g. biology textbooks, journals, articles, film-loops (videograms) (if available))

### Procedure

(*a*) Examine specimens A–G for evidence of asexual reproduction. By means of annotated drawings, describe how asexual reproduction occurs in each organism.

(*b*) Using the information sources provided, copy and complete figure 34 for all specimens.

Show this work to your tutor.

## 2.4 Asexual reproduction in angiosperms — vegetative propagation

The majority of flowering plants reproduce sexually, producing seeds which grow into new individuals. Many flowering plants, however, are also able to reproduce asexually, producing outgrowths which survive and develop after the parent plant has died. These specialised regions of the parent plant are called **organs of vegetative propagation.**

34    **Table for completion**

| Specimen | Major group or phylum | Subgroup or class | Name | Method of asexual reproduction | Main structures concerned |
|---|---|---|---|---|---|
| A | Bryophyta | Hepaticae | Liverwort | By gemmae | Lens-shaped mass of cells in cupules on thallus |
| B | | | | | |

## AV 2 Vegetative propagation

This video sequence shows a range of examples of organs of vegetative propagation.

### Materials

VCR and monitor
ABAL video sequence — *Vegetative propagation*
worksheets

### Procedure

(*a*) Check that you have all the relevant materials for this activity.
(*b*) Check that the video cassette is set up ready to show the appropriate sequence, *Vegetative propagation*.
(*c*) Start the VCR and stop it to complete the worksheets as indicated in the film.
(*d*) If you do not understand anything, stop the video, rewind, and study the relevant material again before consulting your tutor.
(*e*) If possible, work through the video and worksheets with a small group and discuss the material with your fellow students.

## Practical F: Perennating organs in angiosperms

In some plants, the organ of vegetative reproduction is well supplied with stored food reserves. These organs are known as **perennating organs** and enable the plant to continue through the winter period when the aerial parts have died down. Many herbaceous perennials and biennials possess perennating organs. In some cases, perennating organs may also be organs of vegetative reproduction because they possess buds which will give rise to new plants in the spring.

### Materials

6 perennating organs, razor blade or scalpel, hand lens, white tile, test-tubes and rack, test-tube holder, Bunsen burner and tripod stand, pestle and mortar, 500 cm³ beaker, iodine/KI solution, Benedict's reagent, safety glasses

### Procedure

(*a*) Examine each of the specimens provided and attempt to identify which part of the plant has given rise to the organ of perennation/vegetative reproduction. It may be necessary to dissect some organs longitudinally in order to understand their structure.
(*b*) Using the descriptions in figure 35, identify each type of organ provided. Make annotated drawings of one of each named type of organ of perennation/vegetative reproduction. Name also the plant to which it belongs.

Look carefully for the features you would normally associate with a stem or root, e.g. nodes and internodes, axillary buds, scale leaves, terminal buds, absorptive roots, adventitious roots, etc.
(*c*) Using the reagents provided, carry out tests to identify the main types of food stored in each case. Write a full report of your investigations including an account of the methods you used.

Show this work to your tutor.

### 35   Perennating organs in angiosperms

| Name of perennating organ | Origin of organ | Region of food storage |
|---|---|---|
| Bulb | Short, vertical stem | Swollen leaf bases, attached to the vertical stem |
| Corm | Short, vertical stem | Swollen stem base |
| Rhizome | Horizontal stem | Entire length of horizontal stem |
| Stem tuber | Horizontal stem | At tip of stem only |
| Swollen tap root | Main tap root | Entire length of root |
| Root tuber | Root | At tip of root only |

## 2.5 Summary assignment 4

In this section you have learnt about these organs of vegetative reproduction: runner-stolon, sucker, offset, bulb, corm, stem tuber, root tuber, rhizome. Draw up a table to provide the following information for each organ:
plant example (common name and scientific name);
modification involved;
whether it is also a perennating organ;
food storage and type of food.

Show this work to your tutor.

## 2.6 Applications of vegetative propagation

Many of the vegetative structures described in section 2.4 also have a commercial use. The production of bulbs and corms for sale to gardeners and houseplant enthusiasts is one application with which you will be familiar.

Many other plants sold in shops and garden centres are grown from cuttings which produce roots, or plantlets produced in other asexual ways. This is particularly true of plants sold for their decorative foliage.

Potatoes are a staple item of food. 'Seed potatoes' are, in fact, specially set aside tubers with a number of axillary buds.

Fruit-growing has become a very competitive industry, particularly with the expansion of the Common Market. Apples, for example, have to meet very stringent criteria if they are to be successfully produced commercially.

AV 3 *Vegetative propagation and today's world* studies these and other economically important aspects of plant propagation.

---

### AV 3 Vegetative propagation and today's world

---

### Materials

VCR and monitor
ABAL video sequence — *Vegetative propagation and today's world*
worksheets

### Procedure

(*a*) Check that you have all the relevant materials for this activity.
(*b*) Check that the video cassette is set up ready to show the appropriate sequence, *Vegetative propagation and today's world*.
(*c*) Start the VCR and stop it to complete the worksheets as indicated in the film.
(*d*) If you do not understand anything, stop the video, rewind, and study the relevant material again before consulting your tutor.
(*e*) If possible, work through the video and worksheets with a small group and discuss the material with your fellow students.

---

Self test 3, page 108, covers section 2 of this unit.

# Section 3  Sexual reproduction

## 3.1 Introduction and objectives

The first living organisms are believed to have reproduced themselves asexually. However, when life was still at a very primitive level it seems likely that sexual methods of reproduction also evolved. Asexual reproduction ensured the spread of organisms under favourable conditions but sexual reproduction may have provided a means of survival for the species in unfavourable or changing conditions. Offspring that differed genetically from the parent organism might have been better adapted to the different conditions and therefore had a greater chance of survival.

Sexual reproduction in unicellular organisms may occur as a result of the union between two entire organisms but in multicellular organisms (and some unicellular ones) a new individual arises from the fusion of two sex cells, or **gametes.** Each gamete contains a set of chromosomes containing hereditary information in the form of DNA. In most organisms, the male gamete, the **sperm,** consists of little more than a nucleus and a flagellum. The flagellum enables the sperm to swim. The female gametes, **eggs,** are larger than sperm, contain food supplies and are not able to move actively. Animal gametes are produced by **gonads.** The male gonad is the **testis** and the female gonad is the **ovary.** Lower plants are similar to animals in producing eggs and sperm. Eggs are contained in **oogonia** or **archegonia,** while sperm are produced by **antheridia.** Gymnosperms and angiosperms reproduce sexually by means of pollen grains containing the male gamete and ovules containing the female gamete.

The fusion of two gametes is called **fertilisation** and results in one cell called a **zygote** or fertilised egg. The zygote inherits a mixture of hereditary information, half from the egg and half from the sperm. This combination of hereditary information may or may not be advantageous to the offspring which develop from the zygote.

After working through this section you should be able to do the following:
(*a*) List the essential features of sexual reproduction.
(*b*) Understand and define the terms: diploid, haploid, gamete, heterogamete, isogamete, gonads, fertilisation, dioecious, monoecious, hermaphrodite, parthenogenesis, zygote.
(*c*) Describe meiotic cell division and explain its importance in the production of gametes.
(*d*) Give an account of gametogenesis in mammals.
(*e*) Recognise the gametes of animals and flowering plants.
(*f*) Distinguish between external and internal fertilisation.
(*g*) Briefly state the genetic consequences of fertilisation.

## 3.2 Essential features of sexual reproduction

For sexual reproduction to occur, four main events must take place.

— The organism must develop and **mature** sexually. All species require a period of development from the first moment of the existence of a new organism until sexual reproduction can occur.

— **Gametogenesis** must take place. This production of sex cells involves a special type of cell division known as **meiosis** during which the chromosome number is halved.

— The liberation or dispersal of at least one type of gamete (generally referred to as the male gamete). Sometimes both gametes are released.

— The coming together of two gametes of different types (the male and female) and the production of a zygote by the process of fertilisation.

The last three of these processes will be developed more fully in the sub-sections which follow.

## 3.3 Meiosis

The cells of every species of organism have a characteristic number of chromosomes in the nucleus. For example, in human cells there are forty-six, in the cells of fruit-flies, eight, and in crayfish, two hundred. In organisms which reproduce sexually, the cells of each new individual develop from a one-celled stage, the zygote.

In the zygote, half the chromosomes have come from the egg and half have come from the sperm.

The chromosomes exist in pairs, one of each pair being maternal and the other being paternal.

Each of these pairs of chromosomes is called a **homologous pair.** Cells with a complete set of homologous pairs contain the **diploid** (or **2n**) number of chromosomes.

If human sperm and eggs each had the diploid number of chromosomes, a resulting zygote would have ninety-two chromosomes. After a few generations of doubling the chromosome number like this, there would be no room left in a cell for anything apart from chromosomes!

This increase in chromosome number is prevented by a type of cell division called **meiosis.** As a result of meiosis, the chromosome number of a cell is halved, that is, it becomes **haploid** (or **n**). In animals, meiosis occurs during the production of gametes. In plants, meiosis occurs either after zygote formation (in some algae and fungi) or in spore formation (in the higher plants). In all organisms, however, the process of meiosis is remarkably similar.

Figure 36 is a diagrammatic representation of a cell before undergoing meiosis together with the products of meiosis. For simplicity, only two pairs of chromosomes have been drawn in the nucleus and the chromosomes contributed by one parent have been drawn in black and those from the other in white.

**36   Summary of meiosis**

*(a)* **Cell before meiosis**        *(b)* **Products of meiosis**

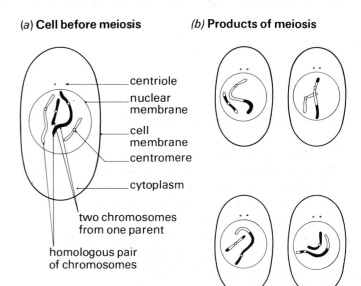

centriole
nuclear membrane
cell membrane
centromere
cytoplasm
two chromosomes from one parent
homologous pair of chromosomes

Study figure 36 carefully and then answer the questions which follow.

*SAQ 27* What is the *total* number of chromosomes (*a*) before, and (*b*) after meiosis?

*SAQ 28* What is the number of chromosomes *per cell* (*a*) before meiosis, (*b*) after meiosis?

*SAQ 29* Compare the genetic make-up of the chromosomes (*a*) before meiosis, (*b*) after meiosis.

*SAQ 30* Using your answers to SAQ 27–29, explain the events which must occur during meiosis to account for the differences in chromosomes before and after meiosis.

During meiosis, the pairs of homologous chromosomes first come together and then separate, as the parent cell divides into two new cells. As a result, each of the new cells will contain the haploid number of chromosomes. This first meiotic division is called a **reduction division** for this reason. During the process of coming together and separating, portions of the chromosomes may be exchanged, a process called **crossing-over.** Maternal and paternal chromosomes are randomly distributed to the daughter cells. This distribution of chromosomes is described as **independent assortment.** As a result, the genetic material becomes mixed. The two haploid

## 37 Changes in DNA content during meiosis

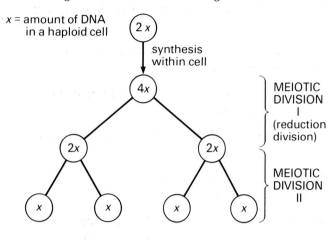

x = amount of DNA in a haploid cell

synthesis within cell

MEIOTIC DIVISION I (reduction division)

MEIOTIC DIVISION II

cells produced by the reduction division immediately undergo a second division essentially similar to mitosis, which results in the final product of four haploid cells.

Figure 37 explains why it is necessary to have two divisions within meiosis. Following a mitotic cell division, a cell will have an amount of DNA which may be represented as $2x$. During the synthetic phase of the cell cycle the amount of DNA doubles ($4x$). The first meiotic division halves the amount of DNA ($2x$) but *complete* chromosomes are present. The second meiotic division again halves the amount of DNA by separating the paired chromatids which constituted each chromosome and one quarter of the original DNA remains ($x$).

## 38 Gametogenesis in animals

### Testis spermatogenesis

### Ovary oogenesis

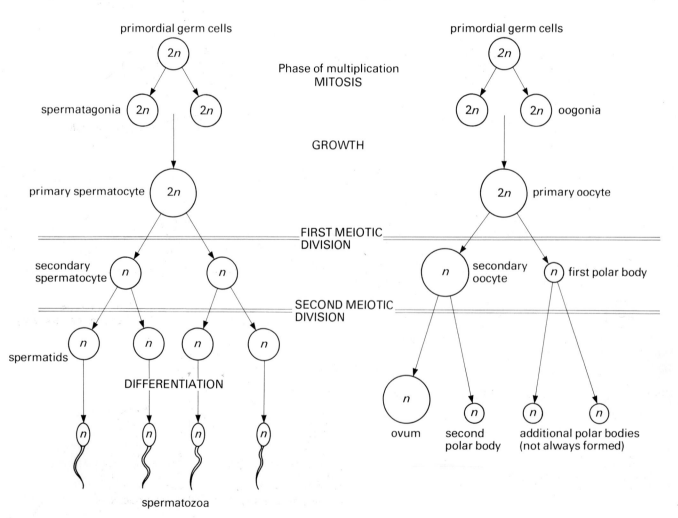

It is important to realise that meiosis is a rare event. It takes place at *only one stage* in the life-cycle of a sexually-reproducing organism.

Meiosis is covered in more detail in the unit *Genetics*.

## 3.4 Gametogenesis (the production of sex cells)

The end-products of meiosis are not yet fully developed sex cells.

In plants, it is mitosis that finally leads to gamete formation. In animals, the meiotic products develop directly into gametes through growth and/or differentiation. The entire process of producing mature gametes is called **gametogenesis**. Gametogenesis in animals is summarised in figure 38.

Study this diagram carefully and answer the following questions.

*SAQ 31* Write down the names of the male and female cells produced by mitosis.

*SAQ 32* Write down the names of the first haploid cells.

*SAQ 33* How does the second meiotic division differ from the first meiotic division?

*SAQ 34* Briefly summarise the main differences between production of gametes in the testis and the ovary.

**39   Gametogenesis in flowering plants**

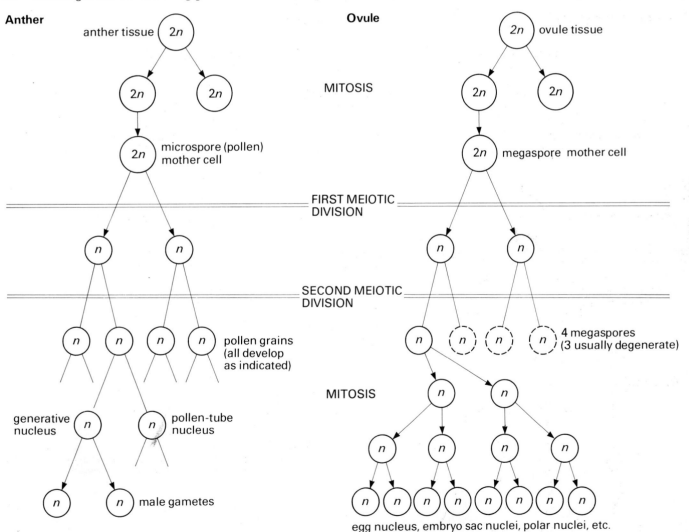

**SAQ 35** Which types of cell are produced by growth processes?

In flowering plants, the male reproductive organ is the **anther** and the female, the **ovary.** Both these structures are contained within the flower (see section 5). Figure 39 shows gametogenesis in flowering plants.

The unfamiliar terms used here will be explained fully in section 5.4.

Compare the pattern of gamete production in flowering plants with that of animals and answer the following questions.

**SAQ 36** Which cells are equivalent to the primary spermatocyte and primary oocyte?

**SAQ 37** How does the pattern of gamete production in plants appear different to that drawn for animal gametogenesis?

Plant reproductive structures such as flowers are produced by cell differentiation at a late stage of the plant life history. In mammals, the testes and ovaries appear during embryonic development though they are not functional until maturity. At birth, the human female possesses her full complement of primary oocytes held at prophase of the first meiotic division. Between puberty and menopause, some hundreds of these are likely to mature and be shed from the ovary. By contrast, the production of spermatozoa does not begin until puberty but may continue throughout life.

## 3.5 Gametes

Figure 40 shows the structure of a mammalian oocyte and also gives an indication of the relative sizes of ovum and sperm. Ova have diameters between 70 and 250 $\mu$m. The total lengths of sperm vary between 40 and 250 $\mu$m.

**41   A mammalian ovum**

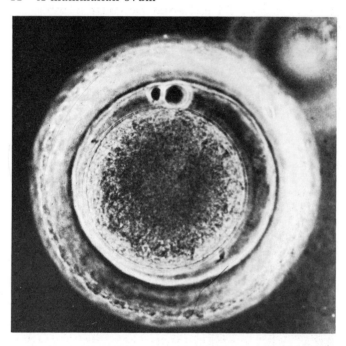

Figure 41 is a photograph of a mammalian ovum. Two polar bodies can be seen to the left of the ovum itself, enclosed by the zona pellucida and surrounding follicle cells.

Because eggs and sperm are so different in appearance, they are called **hetero**gametes. The gametes of some organisms (e.g. *Chlamydomonas*) are identical in appearance and are called **iso**gametes. The gametes of most species of *Chlamydomonas* are motile and swim freely before meeting in pairs and conjugating to produce the zygote. See figure 42.

Some *Chlamydomonas* individuals belong to what is called a plus strain producing plus gametes and these will only conjugate with individuals belonging to a

**40   A mammalian oocyte**

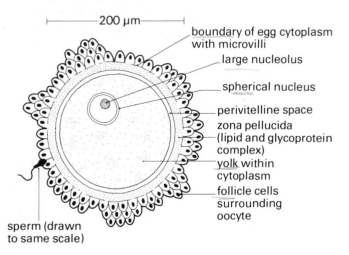

├──── 200 µm ────┤

- boundary of egg cytoplasm with microvilli
- large nucleolus
- spherical nucleus
- perivitelline space
- zona pellucida (lipid and glycoprotein complex)
- yolk within cytoplasm
- follicle cells surrounding oocyte

sperm (drawn to same scale)

minus strain. The two strains differ in the nature of their chemical secretions. It is not possible to assign these gametes to a male or female sex as in higher plants and animals because they are both motile, similar in size and contribute equally to the zygote.

Multicellular animals and simple plants produce small, motile male gametes (sperm) and larger, non-motile, female gametes (ova). The appearance of the spermatozoa varies but, in general, consists of the head, the nucleus containing DNA and a tail or flagellum which brings about movement. Some plant sperm have several flagella and the sperm of some parasites is amoeboid in form. Figure 43 shows human sperm under the electron microscope and figure 44 is a drawing to show details of sperm structure.

Study figures 40 and 44 carefully.

**42** *Chlamydomonas* isogametes

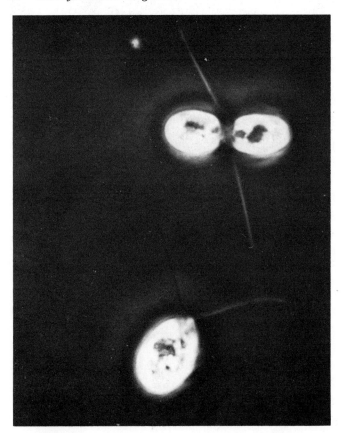

**43** **EM human spermatozoa**

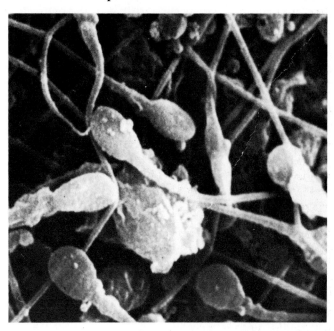

**44** **The structure of a human spermatozoon**

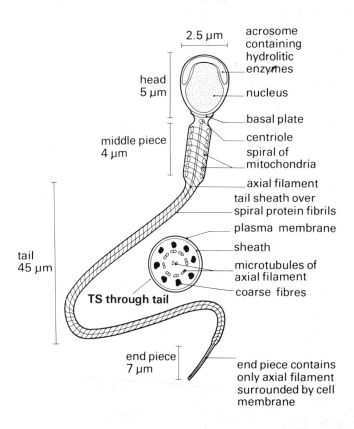

**SAQ 38** List all the differences you can find between the appearance of the sperm and that of the ovum.

**SAQ 39** Suggest a reason for the difference in size between ovum and sperm.

**SAQ 40** (*a*) State concisely the functions of a sperm. (*b*) Explain how its structure is adapted to fulfil these functions.

A woman produces one egg per month from puberty to the end of fertile life (**menopause**) — a period of about thirty years. A normal man liberates around 200 000 000 cells in one ejaculation.

**SAQ 41** Relate the difference in structure of eggs and sperm to the difference in their numbers.

Flowering plants also produce heterogametes. The male gamete is not motile but relies on external agents such as wind or insects for dispersal inside pollen grains. Consider figure 39 once more. This will show you that the pollen grain is not itself the actual gamete. The true gametes are produced from the generative nucleus by mitosis and, in fact, are nuclei only.

Similarly, although the female ovule might seem to correspond to the ovum of an animal, only one of the nuclei contained inside it is actually the female gamete. The gametes of flowering plants will be studied in greater detail in section 5 of this unit.

---

**Practical G: Looking at gametes**

---

In this practical, you will be using sporocarps from the fern, *Marsilea vestita* which grows on mud in shallow ponds and ditches. Figure 45 shows the life-cycle of this fern. Study it carefully before beginning this practical, particularly the stages of the cycle between the germination of the sporocarp and fertilisation.

**Materials**

dried sporocarp of *Marsilea,* demonstration petri dish containing germinating sporocarps, binocular microscope, monocular microscope, slides and coverslips, teat pipette

**Procedure**

(*a*) Examine the demonstration petri dish in which a sporocarp of *Marsilea* has been placed in water. Compare it with a dried sporocarp. Use the binocular microscope for your initial observations.
(*b*) What has happened to (i) the size and (ii) the internal contents of the sporocarp?
(*c*) Look for the two types of spore in the sori.
(*d*) Using a pipette, transfer a few drops of water containing megaspores and microspores onto a slide. Add a coverslip. Examine the slide under low power and high power of a monocular microscope.
(*e*) Compare the germinated and non-germinated forms. Notice the neck of the archegonium protruding from the germinated megaspores.
(*f*) Look for male gametes released from the microspores. Where do they appear to be aggregated? Suggest reasons for this.
(*g*) Make a diagram to show the structure of the male gametes and describe the way in which they move.

Show this work to your tutor.

If you wish to follow the life-cycle of the fern, carry out the following procedure:

(*a*) Leave the developing plants in a covered petri dish in a warm, shady place. After 3–4 days, examine the megaspores to see if fertilisation has occurred. If it has, the female gametophyte will have changed shape from its original form. Make a drawing of this and each subsequent stage in the development of the fern.
(*b*) After 5–6 days, examine the female gametophyte for the presence of rhizoids.
(*c*) After 7–9 days, examine the female gametophyte for the presence of a green cotyledon in the developing embryo. Two days later, examine for the presence of a white root.
(*d*) The developing embryos can be kept in the petri dishes for 3–4 weeks. After this, they should be transferred to an aquarium containing a 2 cm layer of sterilised potting compost. Add water to a level just below the soil surface and cover with a polythene

sheet to maintain humid conditions. Leave the aquarium in a shady place and follow the development of the sporophyte generation.

More information about the life-cycle of ferns is supplied in section 6 of this unit.

### 45  Life-cycle of *Marsilea*

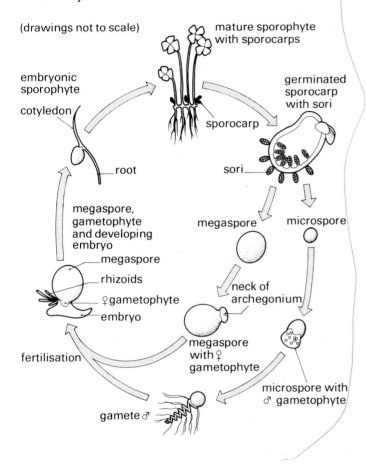

(drawings not to scale)

mature sporophyte with sporocarps

embryonic sporophyte

cotyledon

germinated sporocarp with sori

sporocarp

root

sori

megaspore, gametophyte and developing embryo

megaspore

microspore

megaspore

rhizoids

neck of archegonium

♀ gametophyte

embryo

fertilisation

megaspore with ♀ gametophyte

microspore with ♂ gametophyte

gamete ♂

## 3.6 Fertilisation

**Fertilisation** is defined simply as the fusion of two gametes resulting in the single-celled zygote. The two haploid nuclei join together to restore the diploid number of chromosomes. In this same process, the development of a new individual is initiated.

Among animals, fertilisation is described as being either external or internal.

**External fertilisation** is the most usual method of fertilisation for aquatic animals. The ova and sperm are released into the water and the sperm swim to the ova. Chemical attraction is thought to be involved. The chances of the sperm reaching the ova are greatly increased by a variety of mechanisms. Among the simpler invertebrates, the release of gametes is carefully coordinated by rhythms related to the tides, the moon's cycle or day length. Chemicals (pheromones) released into the water synchronise the release of gametes in some species. Courtship behaviour carried out by males and females of some species of fish, e.g. the stickleback, also leads to the release of gametes in a way that increases the chances for the union of egg and sperm.

More details of external fertilisation in animals will be found in section 6 of this unit.

The process of fertilisation in the lower plants, including pteridophytes, is also partly external and dependent on the presence of water or, at least, a thin film of moisture. The sperm may swim in the moisture following gradients of chemicals emitted by the female organs.

Fertilisation in mosses and ferns, plants that have become adapted to some extent to life on land, occurs within the female archegonium.

You may have seen some evidence of the process of fertilisation in *Marsilea* while working through practical G. Further information about reproduction in mosses and ferns will be found in sections 6 and 8 of this unit.

Most terrestrial organisms have evolved methods of **internal fertilisation.** Here, fertilisation occurs within the female organism and the fertilised zygotes are often retained inside some portion of the female reproductive tract until they complete part of their development. A variety of methods are used to deliver sperm into the female reproductive tract. In some arthropods, the sperm are enclosed inside a packet or spermatophore which is inserted into the female genital tract by either the male or female.

Male sharks and rays possess modified pelvic fins — claspers — which aid transfer of sperm to the female genital opening. The courtship displays of birds end in the pressing together of the male and female cloacas, while insects, mammals and some reptiles have developed a special organ to aid transfer of male gametes, the penis.

Gymnosperms and angiosperms have also evolved a method of internal fertilisation though the process of pollination which precedes fertilisation involves similar risks to external fertilisation.

The process of external fertilisation is a relatively wasteful one. Large numbers of gametes are produced in order that a few zygotes may develop into mature organisms. Internal fertilisation increases the chances of fertilisation. A period of internal development or parental care also increases the chances of survival.

The life-spans of most gametes are limited. Eggs that are shed into the water — those of most invertebrates, fish and amphibians, must be fertilised within a few minutes. To increase the chance of fertilisation, the number of sperm must exceed the number of eggs.

The **acrosome** at the tip of the sperm 'head' contains lytic enzymes which enable the sperm head to penetrate the outer layers of the ovum. The egg nucleus now finishes its second meiotic division and a polar body is again produced. The acrosomal membrane breaks down as it contacts the outer layer of the egg cell and the sperm nucleus moves towards the nucleus of the ovum. Changes occur in the egg cell membranes that cause it to resist the entry of all other sperm. The haploid egg and sperm nuclei unite. DNA synthesis and chromosome replication has occurred and the newly-formed diploid zygote is ready for cleavage (see section 9).

---

## AV 4 Fertilisation

---

### Materials

VCR and monitor
ABAL video sequence — *Fertilisation*
worksheets

### Procedure

(*a*) Check that you have all the relevant materials for this activity.

(*b*) Check that the video cassette is set up ready to show the appropriate sequence, *Fertilisation*.
(*c*) Start the VCR and stop it to complete the worksheets as indicated in the film.
(*d*) If you do not understand anything, stop the video, rewind, and study the relevant material again before consulting your tutor.
(*e*) If possible, work through the video and worksheets with a small group and discuss the material with your fellow students.

---

## 3.7 *Extension:* Egg numbers

46    Vertebrate egg numbers

| Animal | Eggs produced at one time |
|---|---|
| Cod | 3 000 000–7 000 000 |
| Herring | 30 000 |
| Frog | 1000–2000 |
| Adder | 10–14 |
| Pheasant | 14 |
| Thrush | 4-5 |
| Dog | 4 |
| Man | 1 |

Figure 46 gives information on the number of eggs provided by a variety of vertebrate animals. Examine the table and, using reference books where necessary, account for the numbers of eggs produced by each of the organisms named. You will need to consider factors such as the chances of successful fertilisation, the degree of protection for eggs and developing young, the risks involved in the habitat of the young animal. This information should be produced in essay form and handed to your tutor for marking. (The actual writing of the essay, once the information has been gathered, should not take longer than forty minutes.)

Show this work to your tutor.

## 3.8 Hermaphroditism and the monoecious state

**Hermaphroditism** in animals and the **monoecious** state in plants are terms used to describe the situation when both male and female reproductive organs are present in the same individual. Monoecious plants may either have both male and female organs in the same flower (**bisexual flowers**) or have separate male and female flowers (**unisexual flowers**).

Among animals, hermaphrodites occur mainly in the coelenterates, molluscs, annelids and some crustaceans and fish. They are also fairly common among endoparasites. Most hermaphrodite animals are found to be sessile or slow-moving. For example, snails and barnacles are hermaphrodite but faster-moving members of the same phyla such as squid and crabs, have separate sexes.

**SAQ 42** Explain the advantages of hermaphroditism to sessile or slow-moving animals.

**SAQ 43** Suggest a reason why most flowering plants are monoecious.

Plants that have separate male and female individuals are said to be **dioecious.**

Most hermaphrodite animals and monoecious plants do not self-fertilise. Many possess adaptations to ensure cross-fertilisation.

**SAQ 44** Give a reason why self-fertilisation might not benefit a species.

**SAQ 45** Consult a zoology or biology textbook to discover how earthworms ensure cross-fertilisation. Write down an outline account of the process. Suitable reference books would include: *Animal Biology,* Grove and Newell; *Plant and Animal Biology,* vol. I, Vines and Rees; *Animals without Backbones,* Ralph Buchsbaum; *Zoology,* Chapman and Barker.

## 3.9 Parthenogenesis

Parthenogenesis takes place when an ovum develops into a new individual without fertilisation. This process occurs commonly among the arthropods. It is usually combined in the life history with a normal sexual phase of reproduction.

The queen honey-bee is capable of laying either fertilised or unfertilised eggs which hatch as diploid or haploid larvae. Diploid larvae will be females, either workers or queens and the haploid larvae become male 'drones'.

Aphids also reproduce parthenogenetically. In summer, female aphids produce successive generations of diploid parthenogenetic females. The last generations of the season contains males also. Sexual reproduction then occurs to produce an over-wintering generation of eggs that hatch in spring.

**SAQ 46** Consider the mode of life of aphids. Why is parthenogenesis a useful method of reproduction for them?

**SAQ 47** Give two advantages for having a sexual stage in the life-cycle.

*Daphnia* is another organism that has a parthenogenetic reproductive stage in its life history and also a stage of normal sexual reproduction.

**SAQ 48** Suggest the conditions under which *Daphnia* might reproduce (*a*) parthenogenetically, (*b*) sexually.

**SAQ 49** Do you consider that parthenogenesis should be described as asexual or sexual reproduction. Justify your answer.

Artificial pricking of eggs with a needle under laboratory conditions can initiate cleavage (division) of the eggs in the absence of sperm. Most embryos die in early stages but some amphibian eggs have developed into adult animals.

**SAQ 50** Are these animals likely to reproduce normally? Explain your answer.

## 3.10 Summary assignment 5

Section 3 contains a specialised vocabulary. In your notebook write a brief explanation or definition of each of the words or phrases listed below:
diploid, haploid, gamete, isogamete, heterogamete, gonad, fertilisation (external and internal), zygote, dioecious, monoecious, hermaphrodite, meiosis, gametogenesis, parthenogenesis.

Show this work to your tutor.

Self test 4, page 108, covers section 3 of this unit.

# Section 4 Reproduction in mammals

## 4.1 Introduction and objectives

In section 3.6, it was seen that fertilisation in most terrestrial organisms is internal and that this method increases the chances of successful production of zygotes. As animals became better adapted for life on land, many of them retained the developing embryos within the shelter of the body of the female for longer periods. This evolutionary trend is well illustrated among the mammals.

Mammals need a relatively long period of development and, because they are warm-blooded, they need a plentiful food supply from the beginning of their life. All mammals have developed methods of providing more food than can be stored within the confines of an egg.

**Monotremes,** the duck-billed platypus and spiny anteater, lay shelled eggs like the reptiles and birds but when these eggs hatch, the mother produces milk on which the young are nourished while continuing their development. The young of **marsupials** such as the opossums and kangaroos are born after a very short period inside the body of the mother and while still in a very early stage of development. They travel up to a pouch formed by the mother's skin. Within the pouch they attach to a teat through which they are supplied with milk.

Most mammals retain their young within a uterus where they are nourished by means of a placenta connecting the developing embryo indirectly with the blood supply of the mother. Nutrients and oxygen carried by the blood of the mother diffuse across into the blood of the embryo and waste products are removed from the embryo by the same process. After birth, food continues to be available to the young in the form of milk.

This section looks more closely at sexual

reproduction in **eutherian** or true placental mammals, studying the structural and physiological adaptations necessary to bring about internal fertilisation and development and the continued care of the young mammal from birth until it is able to live a fully independent life. Human beings are eutherian mammals and it is their reproductive processes that will be studied wherever possible.

After working through this section you should be able to do the following:
(a) Define the following terms: gonad, puberty, oestrous cycle, oestrus, copulation or coitus, implantation, extra embryonic membranes, gestation, parturition, lactation.
(b) Identify the urinogenital structures of male and female mammals.
(c) Relate gametogenesis to the structure of the ovary and testis.
(d) List the main developments which occur at sexual maturation.
(e) Give an account of the stages of the menstrual cycle.
(f) Explain how the menstrual cycle is regulated by hormones.
(g) Describe how mating and fertilisation are achieved.
(h) Describe the structures and functions of the placenta.
(i) Name the hormones that regulate pregnancy and birth.
(j) Explain the changes that take place in the blood circulation of a baby at and around the time of birth.
(k) Give an account of birth and subsequent parental care in mammals.

## 4.2 The urinogenital system of a mammal

Although the renal and reproductive systems are

concerned with different activities and arise separately in the course of development, their ducts are intimately connected in the adult animal, particularly in the male. Thus, the structures are necessarily examined together though the functions are studied separately. (Nitrogenous excretion is considered in the unit *Exchange and transport*.) The combined structures are known as the **urinogenital system.**

---

## Practical H: The urinogenital system of a mammal

---

### Materials

Small mammal or dissected mammal, dissection kit (scalpel, scissors, seeker, needles, forceps), *Dissection guides. III. The Rat:* H.G.Q. Rowett, dissection dish or board, pins

### Procedure

(*a*) Either
(i) dissect the mammal provided to show the urinogenital system. Refer to relevant pages in your dissection guide. Or
(ii) examine the dissected rats provided. Use the dissection guide to help you identify the following structures:

| *male* | *female* |
|---|---|
| kidney | kidney |
| ureter | ureter |
| bladder | bladder |
| testis | ovaries |
| scrotum | uterus |
| sperm duct (vas deferens) | oviduct (Fallopian tube) |
| penis | vagina |
| urethra | urethra |

(*b*) Look for the difference between male and female urethra. Note this in your practical book.
(*c*) Make carefully annotated drawings to show male and female reproductive systems.
(*d*) Figures 47 and 48 are diagrams of the human male and female urinogenital systems. Compare these diagrams with the structures present in your dissection.

**47  Section through the pelvis to show human male reproductive organs**

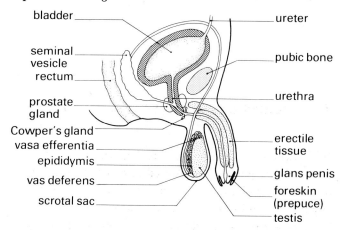

**48  Section through the pelvis to show human female reproductive organs**

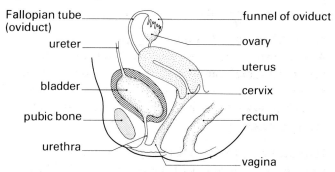

### Discussion of results

1 Which human female organ appears to differ most from the structures in your dissection?
2 List any differences you can observe between the diagram of reproductive structures in the human male and the dissection of the small mammal.

Show this work to your tutor.

## 4.3 The gonads

The primary sexual organs are referred to as gonads. They consist of paired testes which produce male gametes and paired ovaries which produce female gametes.

In most mammals the testes develop in the abdominal cavity but migrate down to the scrotal sacs before birth. The testes are generally maintained

## 49  Diagram of the testis cut vertically

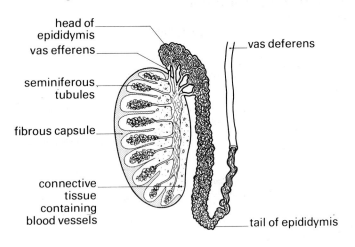

- head of epididymis
- vas efferens
- seminiferous tubules
- fibrous capsule
- connective tissue containing blood vessels
- vas deferens
- tail of epididymis

at a temperature about 5 °C below the core temperature of the body. Spermatogenesis will not take place at body temperature in mammals with scrotal testes.

The human testes are oval structures about 5 cm long. They are divided into about 300 compartments and within each of these lie three coiled **seminiferous tubules.** The total length of these may exceed 200 metres. Figure 49 shows the structure of the testes.

The epididymis is a twisted tube with muscular walls capable of peristaltic contraction. It is about 6 metres long and 1 mm wide. Sperm may be stored here.

If the testis is cut through transversely, its tubular nature can be clearly seen. This is shown in figure

## 50  Section through seminiferous tubules in testis

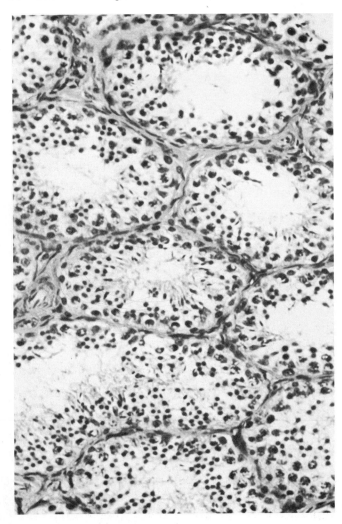

## 51  TS of part of a single seminiferous tubule

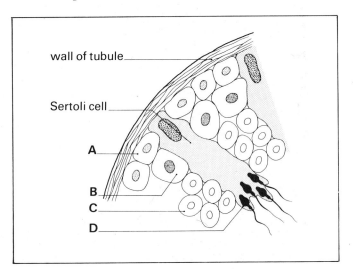

- wall of tubule
- Sertoli cell
- A
- B
- C
- D

50. Figure 51 shows the structure of a single tubule in diagrammatic form. Various cells are identified by letters only. These letters refer to the process of spermatogenesis.

*SAQ 51* With reference to figure 38 in section 3.4. identify the cells labelled **A–D.** (Secondary spermatocytes have a short life and are rarely seen in sections. For this reason, they have not been shown here.)

*SAQ 52* Indicate which cells (**A–D**) will be haploid and which diploid.

*SAQ 53* The testis has a rich blood supply.
(*a*) Why is this necessary?

**52 Section through an ovary**

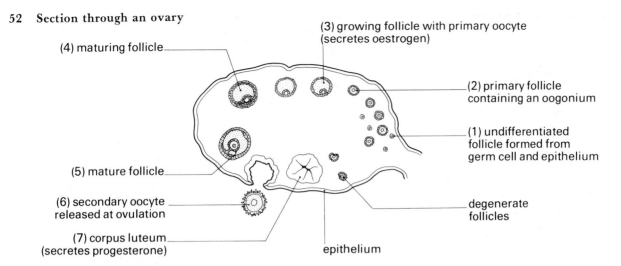

(4) maturing follicle

(3) growing follicle with primary oocyte (secretes oestrogen)

(2) primary follicle containing an oogonium

(1) undifferentiated follicle formed from germ cell and epithelium

(5) mature follicle

(6) secondary oocyte released at ovulation

(7) corpus luteum (secretes progesterone)

degenerate follicles

epithelium

**53 Mature follicle**

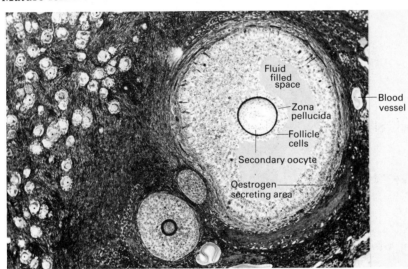

Fluid filled space

Zona pellucida

Follicle cells

Secondary oocyte

Oestrogen secreting area

Blood vessel

(b) In what part of the testis might you expect to find blood vessels?

The ovaries are also oval shaped and about 30 mm long. Figure 52 shows a section through an ovary in diagrammatic style. An ovary consists of a thin outer layer of epithelium. Below this lies a layer of dense connective tissue surrounding the cortex which contains **follicles** in varying stages of development.

A primary follicle consists of a layer of follicle cells (formed from the germinal epithelium) which surrounds the oogonium. The oogonium has the potential of developing into an egg.

At birth, there are up to 400 000 primary follicles in each ovary but only about 200–400 complete their development.

The remainder degenerate into small cyst-like bodies within the ovary and then disappear.

Figure 53 is a photomicrograph of an ovarian follicle.

Each month, one (usually) of the eggs is shed from one of the ovaries during **ovulation.** This process begins at **puberty,** the time of sexual maturation, and continues until the time of menopause when sex hormone levels fall and a female is no longer fertile. Puberty may commence as early as nine years of age or at sixteen years or older. The menopause generally occurs between forty-five and fifty years of age.

**SAQ 54** Name the reproductive cell inside an immature, growing follicle.

**SAQ 55** Name the reproductive cell inside a mature follicle just about to rupture.

**SAQ 56** What other structures are likely to be present within a mature follicle about to rupture.?

---

**Practical I: Histology of ovaries and testes**

**Materials**

prepared slides of testis and ovary, microscope

**Procedure**

(*a*) Examine, draw and label a section through an ovary. You will probably see follicles at different stages of development in the ovary. Figure 52 will help you to interpret the slides.
(*b*) Examine, draw and label a section through the testis.

Figures 49 and 51 will help you interpret this.
(*c*) Using your observations from practical H, record the following information underneath the relevant drawings.
Position of gonad in body.
Route gamete must take from site of production to point where (i) it leaves the body (sperm), (ii) it reaches the uterus (ova).

Show this work to your tutor.

## 4.4 Sexual maturation

Figure 29 in section 1.9.1 shows a growth curve for the human reproductive organs. The curve is very different from other curves shown in the diagram or from a typical growth curve. The size of reproductive organs remains more or less constant until around the age of twelve when a rapid increase occurs. The beginning of this growth is referred to as puberty. This growth is accompanied by a variety of other changes over a period of two or three years. Some of these changes are listed in Figure 54.

**54  Pubertal changes in males and females**

| Male | Female |
| --- | --- |
| Growth of testes and penis and activation of prostate gland | Growth of ovaries, uterus, vagina |
| Growth of pubic hair | Growth of pubic hair |
| Growth of hair under arms | Growth of hair under arms |
| Heavy growth of hair on face | Light growth of hair on face |
| Heavy growth of hair on body | Light growth of hair on body |
| Eruption of second molars | Eruption of second molars |
| Considerable growth of larynx. Change of voice by octave | Slight growth of larynx. Moderate lowering of voice |
| Widening of shoulders. Considerable thickening of muscles | Widening of hips. Slight thickening of muscles |
| Increase in secretion of sweat | Increase in secretion of sweat |
| Sometimes slight and temporary development around breast nipples | Growth and development of breasts |
| Both sexes undergo a 'growth spurt' in height and the female starts to menstruate | |

These changes are under hormonal control. Evidence about the actual levels of hormones secreted is inadequate but suggests that the large increases at puberty are in **oestrogens** and **androgens**. Figure 55 shows data obtained by studying the hormonal activity of extracts of urine per twenty-four hours.

**55 Levels of oestrogen and androgen in urine extracts**

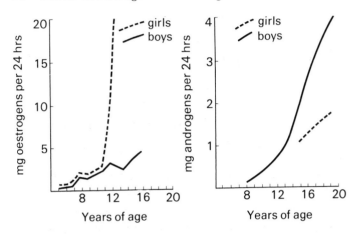

The production of these hormones by the testes, ovary and adrenal gland is under the control of the pituitary gland which secretes hormones stimulating the gonads. These hormones are first secreted in quantity at puberty and continue during the reproductive phase of life. For example, follicle stimulating hormone, FSH, stimulates the female ovaries and in males it stimulates the development of the germinal epithelium of the testes and sperm production. The production of sperm by the testes is a continuous process.

## 4.5 The female sexual cycle

The activity of the ovary shows a regular cycle of egg development and release (ovulation) which is regulated by hormones.

The higher primates (monkeys, apes and humans) together with rats and mice are rather unusual in comparison with other mammals. In all these examples, the sexual cycle of the female continues throughout the year. In other mammals such as cows and sheep, the sexual cycle occurs only during one restricted season of the year which is called the

**breeding season.** Female dogs (bitches) have two breeding seasons per year, during which they undergo one sexual cycle.

Many female mammals 'come on heat' at regular intervals during the breeding season. At these times the female becomes sexually receptive and attractive to males. These periods of heightened sexual activity are called **oestrus** (from the Greek *oistros*, meaning 'gadfly'. Mares in oestrus behave as through they were being stung). Oestrus usually coincides with ovulation (i.e. the time when fertilisation is most likely to occur as a result of mating, or copulation). Human beings are exceptional among animals in being sexually receptive at all times.

For women, the cycle of the ovary is marked by the discharge of blood from the vagina. These regular 'periods' are known as **menstruation** (Latin: *mensis*; month) as they occur approximately every twenty-eight days. As oestrus is the most obvious outward sign of the female sexual cycle, it is known as the oestrous cycle. (Oestrous is the adjective.) In humans, it is called the menstrual cycle.

The menstrual cycle involves changes in the ovaries and the uterus. The main events in the menstrual cycle are summarised in figure 56 which takes the onset of menstruation as its starting point.

*SAQ 57* Figure 57 shows an incomplete summary of the menstrual cycle to show the changes that occur in the ovary and uterus. Make a copy of the table and complete it by filling in the numbered spaces.

## 4.6 Hormonal control of the menstrual cycle

The changes which occur in the ovaries and uterus during the menstrual cycle are controlled by the interactions of a complex of hormones.

Hormones are secreted by endocrine glands directly into the circulating blood to be carried around the body. Hormones act as chemical messengers and the organs which respond to the hormones are referred to as **target organs.** The target organs of the hormones of the menstrual cycle are the ovaries and the lining of the uterine wall, the endometrium.

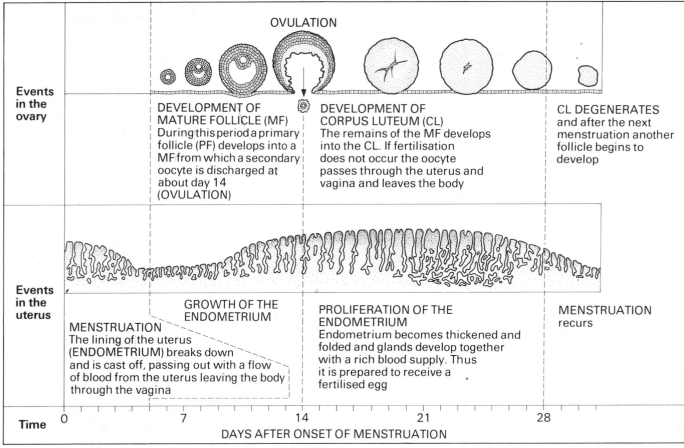

A mature follicle is often referred to as a Graafian follicle after de Graaf who first described it

## 57   Summary of the menstrual cycle

| Time (days) | Events in the ovary | Events in the uterus |
|---|---|---|
| 0 ↓ 4/5 | | (1) ................... occurs |
| 5/6 | (2) ........................... develops into (3) ........ ........................... | (4) ........................... ........................... |
| 14 | (5) ................... occurs | |
| 28 | (6) ........................... develops, but gradually degenerates. | (7) ........................... (8) ................... recurs |

A detailed account of hormone control of body activities is contained in the unit: *Response to the environment*. Only the essential facts are given in this unit. Figure 58 shows the main structures and hormones involved in the menstrual cycle.

The hypothalamus is a part of the brain to which the pituitary gland is attached by a short 'stalk'. It controls the menstrual cycle by secreting **releasing factors** which act on the pituitary, the major endocrine gland of the body, and stimulate it to secrete luteinising hormone (LH) and follicle stimulation hormone (FSH).

Both these hormones stimulate the female gonad (ovary) which can also act as an endocrine gland. For this reason they are known as **gonadotrophic hormones.**

## 58  Hormones of the menstrual cycle

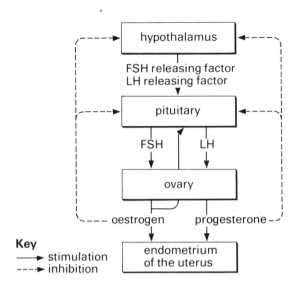

Key
— stimulation
--- inhibition

the blood increase, the follicle cells are stimulated to produce oestrogen. Oestrogen stimulates the repair and growth of the endometrium following menstruation.

FSH also stimulates ovarian tissue to secrete low levels of oestrogen. Thus, during the first two weeks of the cycle the level of oestrogen in the woman's blood increases. See figure 59.

## 59  Events in the first two weeks of the menstrual cycle

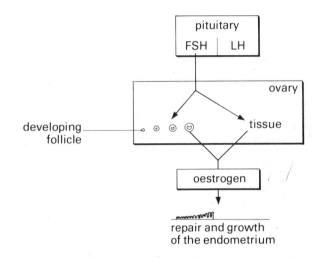

**SAQ 58** (*a*) Which hormone is produced by the ovary in response to (i) luteinising hormone, (ii) follicle stimulating hormone?
(*b*) Which are the target organs of these two hormones?

Progesterone and oestrogen do not only affect the endometrium they **inhibit** (reduce or stop) the secretion of FSH releasing factor and LH releasing factor by the hypothalamus and the secretion of LH and FSH by the pituitary. This role is indicated by the broken lines in figure 58.

**SAQ 59** What series of events will occur as a result of the inhibitory action of progesterone and oestrogen?

The situation whereby the level of hormones circulating in the body is controlled by the inhibitory effect of the hormones themselves is referred to as **negative feedback.** A more detailed account of negative feedback is given in the unit *Response to the environment.*

The production of FSH by the pituitary can be taken as the starting point of the menstrual cycle. Under the influence of FSH the Graafian follicle develops during the first two weeks. As the levels of FSH in

Oestrogen affects the pituitary negatively by inhibiting the production of FSH but it has a positive effect also and high levels of oestrogen stimulate the release of LH. See figure 60.

## 60  The effects of oestrogen

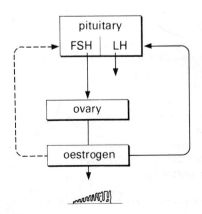

LH brings about the rapid growth of the follicle which leads to **ovulation,** when the follicle opens to release the secondary oocyte.

Under the influence of LH the remains of the Graafian follicle becomes filled with enlarged follicle cells containing a yellow pigment, forming the yellow body called the **corpus luteum** (CL). The corpus luteum stimulated by LH then secretes the hormone progesterone (see figure 61).

**61   The effects of luteinising hormone (LH)**

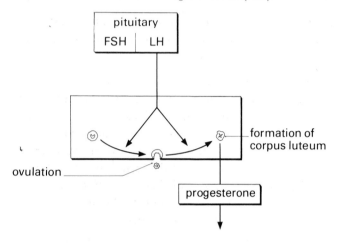

Progesterone stimulates the stage of very rapid growth of the endometrium which is referred to as **proliferation.** It also stimulates activity of the outermost layers of the endometrium which prepares

**62   The effects of progesterone**

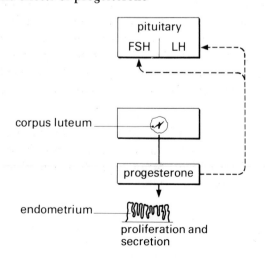

the uterus to receive the developing embryo. Progesterone also inhibits further production of LH and FSH by the pituitary (see figure 62).

*SAQ 60* List the four hormones of the menstrual cycle in the order in which they are produced.

*SAQ 61* List the three functions of oestrogen in the menstrual cycle.

*SAQ 62* List the three functions of LH.

If fertilisation has not occurred, and an embryo has not become implanted in the uterus, the corpus luteum in the absence of LH, degenerates and ceases to secrete progesterone. The proliferated uterine lining breaks down and is sloughed off with a certain amount of blood loss. This process is termed **menstruation** and occurs only in a few groups of the primates. After menstruation, the cycle repeats itself.

*SAQ 63* What is the signal for the resumption of FSH production which sets the cycle in motion again?

## 4.7 Summary assignment 6

To provide a summary of the functions of circulatory reproductive hormones, copy and complete figure 63. Name the events or structures (1) to (6) and add solid or dotted lines for the various hormones

**63   Summary diagram: hormonal control of the menstrual cycle**

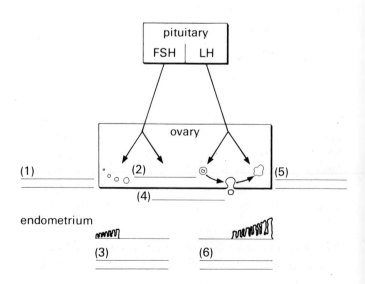

involved to indicate stimulation and inhibition respectively. Your drawings from Practicals H and I and answers to SAQ 51 to 57 summarise sections 4.2 to 4.5.

Show this work to your tutor.

## 4.8 Mating and fertilisation

Mammals show a variety of types of behaviour which precede the act of mating. Courtship is often less elaborate than in birds but some pair-bond, even though very temporary, is usually established before the reproductive act takes place. The essential part of the act of mating is the transfer of sperm from the male into the upper part of the vagina of the female. In some species, the sperm are transferred directly to the uterus.

The process of transfer is referred to as **mating, copulation** or **coitus.** Transfer of sperm is brought about by the **penis.**

64   TS through the penis in mid region

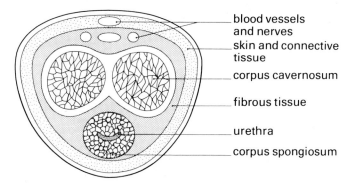

blood vessels and nerves
skin and connective tissue
corpus cavernosum
fibrous tissue
urethra
corpus spongiosum

The penis serves two functions, as a passageway for urine from the bladder and a conveyor of sperm into the female body. Figure 64 shows the urethra, the passage for both urine and sperm. Usually the penis is a soft, flaccid organ and when in this state, urine can be released to the outside if sphincter muscles relax.

The diagram shows that the penis is composed of three cylindrical masses of spongy tissue surrounded by skin. This skin is well supplied with sensitive nerve endings. The penis also receives a rich arterial blood supply. When a male is sexually excited, the artery walls in the penis relax by reflex action and more blood flows in, filling the spaces of the corpus cavernosum. The veins which would nomally carry blood away are reflexly closed by valves. Blood is thus trapped in the penis which expands and becomes erect and firm. In this condition it can be pushed into the vagina of a receptive female which is lubricated with mucus to ease the passage of the penis.

(Before continuing, look back at figures 47 and 48 to make sure that you are familiar with the anatomy of the reproductive systems.)

Sperm are rapidly transported from the vas deferentia (sperm ducts) by muscular contraction into the posterior urethra. The seminal vesicles produce a thick secretion which is added to by the prostate gland as both empty into the posterior urethra and mix with the sperm at **ejaculation.** This occurs when the fluid mixture, now called semen, spurts out through the tip of the penis due to the action of muscles near the base of the penis.

(During ejaculation, a valve automatically closes the opening between the urethra and the bladder.) During coitus, the ejaculation deposits semen containing sperm near the cervix or entrance to the uterus. From here, they will swim or be passively transported through the uterus and into the Fallopian tubes (oviducts) where they may meet an ovum. The chances of an individual human sperm meeting an ovum are very small and this is balanced by the vast number produced. An average ejaculation contains about four hundred million sperm. If this falls below two hundred million, a man is likely to be considered infertile.

The process of fertilisation was considered in section 3.6. It is considered to be complete once the two haploid nuclei have fused to produce a single-celled diploid zygote.

## 4.9 Pregnancy

Figure 65 shows the events of the first week after fertilisation. Cleavage and the subsequent stages of growth of the embryo are studied in greater detail in section 9 of this unit.

**65    Development of a fertilised egg during the first week**

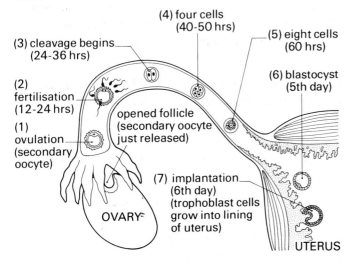

**SAQ 64** How would you expect the embryo to be nourished and acquire oxygen as it moves down the fallopian tube and into the uterus?

**SAQ 65** Name the part of the uterus into which the blastocyst implants itself.

**SAQ 66** How is the uterus prepared to receive the embryo?

**SAQ 67** What part of the blastocyst brings about implantation?

In the uterus development of the original fertilised zygote continues and gives rise to
(*a*) the embryo,
(*b*) the extra embryonic membranes,
(*c*) part of the placenta.

Figure 66 shows the human embryo or **foetus** (as it is called after eight weeks) at three stages of its development.

The extra embryonic membranes begin to form early in development. As these membranes develop, they acquire important roles in protecting and

maintaining the embryo. The extra embryonic membranes are the amnion, the chorion and the allantois.

Figure 67 shows the arrangement of the extra embryonic membranes in relation to embryo and developing placenta. The **amnion** has no blood vessels and consists of two layers of epithelium. They enclose the foetus in a fluid-filled cavity which prevents the embryo from becoming desiccated and acts as a shock absorber.

The **allantois** has a blood supply and grows out of the hind-gut of the embryo. It plays an important role in the nourishment of the foetus.

The **chorion** is also vascularised and is the outermost membrane, also composed of two layers of epithelium.

**66    Three early stages in the development of a human being**

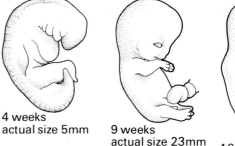

4 weeks
actual size 5mm

9 weeks
actual size 23mm

16 weeks
actual size 160mm

**67    Extra embryonic membranes at an early stage of human development**

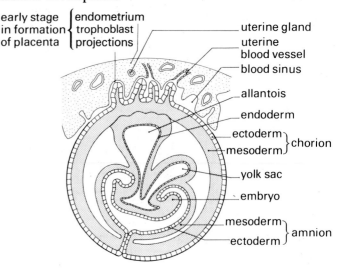

The **placenta** develops at the point of implantation. The trophoblast cells (see figure 67) multiply rapidly and grow deeply into the endometrium. It is this same group of trophoblast cells that give rise also to the extra embryonic membranes.

## 4.9.1 The placenta and its function

At first, the trophoblast cells absorb food and oxygen from the increasingly vascularised uterine lining. The allantois grows out from the embryo and fuses with the chorion to form the allanto-chorion which will develop into the placenta. Finger-like projections or villi grow out into the blood spaces of the uterus lining (see figure 67). These villi eventually branch producing a tree-like structure. Thus, embryonic tissues project directly into the mother's blood sinuses. The villi provide a large surface area (about half the size of a tennis court) for interchange of materials between the embryo and the mother. The allantois gives rise to the umbilical cord which contains blood vessels connecting foetus and placenta. Figure 68 shows the connections between foetus and mother.

**68  Connections between foetus and mother via the placenta**

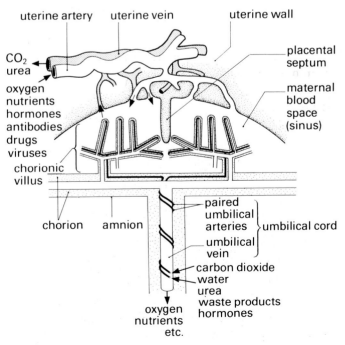

By the twenty-first day of development, the embryo's heart is pumping blood through the already established circulatory system including the blood vessels in the umbilical cord leading to the placenta.

Oxygen, nutrients and other substances present in the blood of the mother diffuse into the placental blood vessels along the diffusion gradients. Similarly, carbon dioxide and other waste products from the foetus diffuse into the blood of the mother. Harmful substances such as drugs and even bacteria and viruses can also pass through the membranes of the placenta.

The haemoglobin present in foetal blood is slightly different in structure and properties from adult haemoglobin. Study figure 69.

**69  Oxygen affinity of foetal and adult haemoglobin**

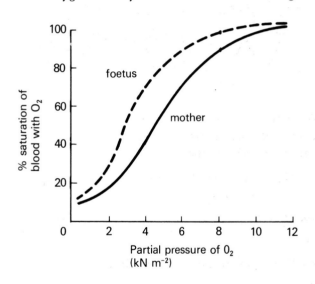

*SAQ 68* Which haemoglobin, foetal or maternal, combines most readily with oxygen at low partial pressures?

*SAQ 69* Uterine partial pressure of oxygen is about 8 kN m$^{-2}$. What is the difference in percentage saturation of $O_2$ between foetal and adult haemoglobin at this point?

*SAQ 70* How will this assist uptake of oxygen by foetal blood at this point?

*SAQ 71* How does the blood in the uterine arteries differ from that in the umbilical arteries?

Figure 70 shows the arrangement of blood vessels in the placenta.

**SAQ 72** Blood at relatively high pressure in maternal blood vessels lies close to blood at lower pressure in foetal vessels and vice versa. How does this arrangement assist the placenta to carry out its functions?

The fact that maternal and foetal blood flow past each other in opposite directions also assists the efficient exchange of materials. Counterflow exchange mechanisms are studied further in the unit *Exchange and transport*.

The foetus is genetically different and therefore its proteins could be detected as immunologically alien and might be expected to lead to rejection of the foetus by the maternal tissues. That this does not occur is considered to be due to a number of delicately balanced mechanisms. Among these is the fact that the placental membranes act as a molecular filter, preventing the interchange of large molecules like proteins.

Recently, however, it has become clear that the placenta does not merely act as a passive filter but can be active and selective in its transfer of substances essential to the development of the foetus.

At the end of pregnancy, the foetus is supplied with antibodies from the mother that will protect it against infection until its own immune system can begin to function. These large protein molecules are conveyed by active and selective transport mechanisms.

Rhesus disease of the newborn (blue babies) is caused by the presence of a baby of the rhesus positive blood group in the uterus of a rhesus negative mother. If, in a previous pregnancy and birth, some of the Rh$^+$ blood cells from the child have entered the mother's circulation, she will have produced antibodies against them. These antibodies may subsequently pass through the placenta in late pregnancy and will destroy some of the red blood cells of the foetus.

Some drugs, bacteria and viruses although consisting of relatively large molecules, also manage to pass

**70  Arrangement of maternal and foetal blood vessels in the placenta**

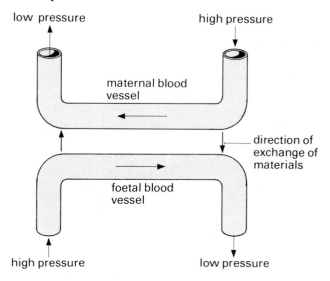

through the placental barrier.

**SAQ 73** From your own knowledge name
(a) one harmful drug, (b) one harmful virus that may pass across the placenta?

The production of hormones to regulate the activities of pregnancy is one of the special functions of the placenta. By means of these hormones, the placenta carries out the functions of the foetus's pituitary gland until it is sufficiently developed. The placenta also regulates all the pregnancy hormones. The role of these hormones will be studied in section 4.12.

The main hormones produced are (a) chorionic gonadotrophin, (b) oestrogens, (c) progesterone, (d) placental lactogen.

**SAQ 74** Which of these hormones maintains the endometrium in its proliferated state?

The placenta is also involved in protein synthesis. The vast quantities of structural proteins needed to build up foetal and placental tissues have to be derived from the mother's blood. The raw materials are in the form of amino acids and polypeptides and must be assembled according to foetal demand. The placenta acts rather like the liver in this respect until the foetal liver is sufficiently developed.

The placenta has a very high rate of metabolism and uses about a third of all the oxygen and glucose supplied to it by the maternal circulation for its own metabolic needs.

## 4.10 Birth or parturition

Childbirth usually occurs about 280 days from the first day of the last menstrual period. The actual human gestation period is about 38 weeks. **Gestation** is the period of embryonic development in the fallopian tube and uterus.

Birth is brought about by powerful contractions of the smooth muscle of the wall of the uterus aided by abdominal contractions. What initiates the onset of labour is not fully understood but possible causes are
(*a*) the age of the placenta;
(*b*) the size of the foetus;
(*c*) a change in hormone balance, more oestrogen and less progesterone.

Childbirth is often referred to as labour for it does involve hard work for the mother and the muscles of the uterus. The function of labour is to allow the uterine contractions to widen the opening of the cervix and force out the baby and the placenta. Labour is divided into three stages:

**71    Baby in uterus**

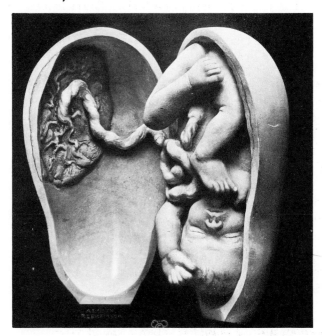

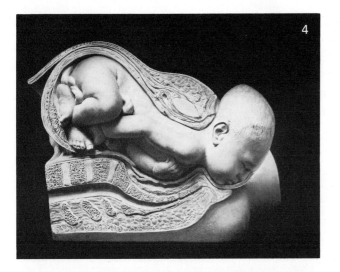

4

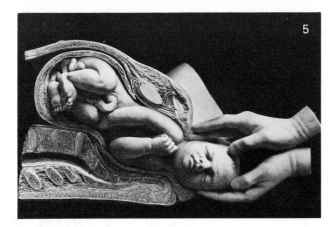

5

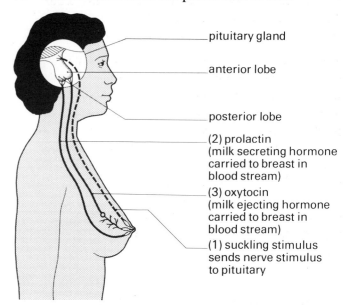

- pituitary gland
- anterior lobe
- posterior lobe
- (2) prolactin (milk secreting hormone carried to breast in blood stream)
- (3) oxytocin (milk ejecting hormone carried to breast in blood stream)
- (1) suckling stimulus sends nerve stimulus to pituitary

(1) The period until the cervix is fully dilated. During this stage, the amniotic sac ruptures and amniotic fluid is released.
(2) The delivery of the child.
(3) The delivery of the placenta.

Figure 71 shows the relationship of uterus, placenta, umbilical cord and baby.

## 4.11 Parental care

The stage of development at which mammals are born varies. Some are well developed and the period for which they are dependent upon the mother after birth is quite short. Many hoofed mammals can run within an hour of their birth. Other mammals are incapable of fending for themselves at birth. The mother must take care of them, keep them warm and provide food for them from her mammary glands. Figure 73 summarises the factors involved in milk production.

Lactation (milk production) is under the control of both nerves and hormones.

*SAQ 75* State the role of nerves in milk release.

*SAQ 76* Name the hormones involved in lactation.

Milk is a complete food for young mammals. It contains dissolved mineral salts, sugar, proteins and fats. Milk varies in composition according to species, as figure 74 shows.

**74 Composition of milk of various species in gl$^{-1}$**

|  | Sugar | Proteins | Fats | Salts |
|---|---|---|---|---|
| Cat | 50 | 92 | 35 | 6 |
| Cow | 45 | 35 | 40 | 9 |
| Dog | 40 | 70 | 85 | 11 |
| Goat | 47 | 33 | 40 | 6 |
| Whale | 4 | 95 | 200 | 10 |
| Woman | 75 | 11 | 35 | 3 |

**SAQ 77** In what two ways does whale milk differ markedly in composition from that of other mammals? Suggest reasons for these differences.

The duration of lactation also varies from a few weeks in a guinea pig to about seven months in whales. In human beings, it depends partly upon how long the baby is allowed to suck. In some primitive tribes mothers suckle their young for two years or more. The amount of care and protection and the length of time a mammal remains with its mother also varies widely. In some cases the males are actively involved in the care of the young and, in others, they play no part. Human beings are dependent upon their parents for longer than any other mammals.

## 4.12 Hormonal control in pregnancy and birth

Before continuing with this topic, revise the hormonal control of the menstrual cycle (section 4.6). Figure 75 summarises the events before pregnancy.

**SAQ 78** (a) What structure causes the rise in oestrogen level after menstruation?
(b) What structure secretes oestrogen during the last two weeks of the menstrual cycle?
(c) From figure 75 and the information in section 4.6, what are the functions and effects of progesterone?
(d) What causes the drop in progesterone if implantation does not occur?
(e) After implantation of the egg, what maintains the high level of progesterone?

A complex of hormones are involved in the control of

**75    The menstrual cycle and pregnancy**

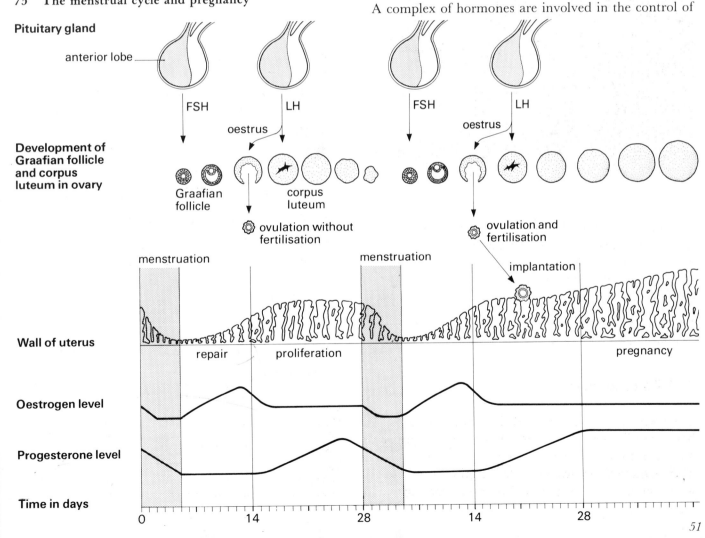

the events during pregnancy, birth and lactation. Figure 76 shows the changes which occur in the level of these hormones circulating in the blood of a human female.

Progesterone inhibits the production of LH at the end of the menstrual cycle. This drop in LH level causes the corpus luteum to degenerate. If implantation occurs, the corpus luteum does not degenerate even though LH levels are still low.

*SAQ 79* Look at figure 76. What hormone is likely to maintain the corpus luteum? Explain your answer.

*SAQ 80* Progesterone levels remain high during pregnancy. What are the two sources of progesterone and what events will cause their changing levels?

The ovary tissue maintains its low level of oestrogen production during pregnancy.

*SAQ 81* What other structure is likely to cause the rapid increase in oestrogen?

The process of **parturition** consists of powerful contractions of the muscular wall of the uterus. As the development of the baby proceeds, its increase in size and more frequent movements stimulate nerve impulses from the uterus to the mother's pituitary. The pituitary secretes a hormone that causes uterine contractions. The action of this hormone is aided by the removal of the inhibitory effect of progesterone on uterine contraction.

**76   Changes in hormone levels following conception**

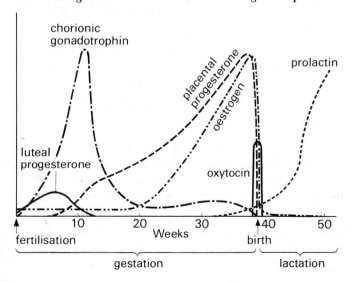

## 77   Summary of the hormones involved in pregnancy, birth and lactation

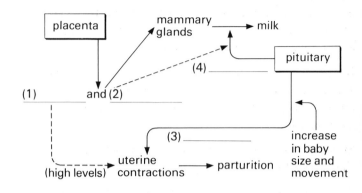

*SAQ 82* Look again at figure 76. What is the name of this hormone?

During the later stages of pregnancy, progesterone and oestrogen stimulate growth of the milk ducts and secretory tissue in the mammary glands.

*SAQ 83* (*a*) Which hormone shown in figure 76 do you think is responsible for the actual production of milk?
(*b*) This hormone is kept at low levels until birth occurs by the inhibitory effect of other hormones. What is the likely inhibitor?

*SAQ 84* Copy and complete the diagram in figure 77 by adding the appropriate hormones (1) to (4).

## 4.13 Summary assignment 7

The following examination question was set by the London Universtiy Board in June 1978.

Describe reproduction in a *named* female mammal. In your answer, refer to sexual cycles, mating, nutrition of the embryo, birth and maternal care. (Diagrams of the female reproductive system are NOT required.)

After planning the essay, you should not spend more than forty-five minutes on writing your answer.

Show this work to your tutor.

Self test 5, page 109, covers section 4 of this unit.

## 4.14 *Extension:* Foetal circulation

The foetus and new-born baby are exposed to very different surroundings. The anatomy and physiology of the baby therefore must undergo rapid change for adjustment to its new environment.

In the case of the circulatory system, a few relatively small anatomical changes at birth result in considerable modification to the function of the circulation.

Study figure 78 very carefully as you work through the account of these changes.

As the foetus cannot eat or breathe, its food and oxygen must be supplied by the mother across the placenta. Flow of blood from the placenta to the foetus will serve as the starting point.

Blood from the placenta goes to the liver of the foetus via the umbilical vein. The **ductus venosus** by-passes the normal circulation of the liver and gut (which is non-functional) and blood enters the general circulation at the vena cava.

**Key**

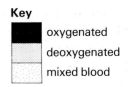

oxygenated
deoxygenated
mixed blood

**After**

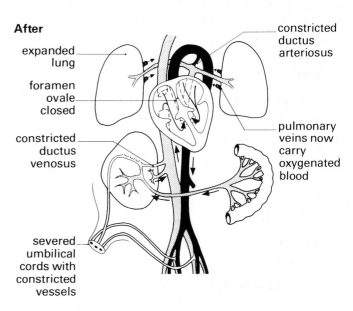

expanded lung

foramen ovale closed

constricted ductus venosus

severed umbilical cords with constricted vessels

constricted ductus arteriosus

pulmonary veins now carry oxygenated blood

**78   Circulation before and after birth**

**Before**

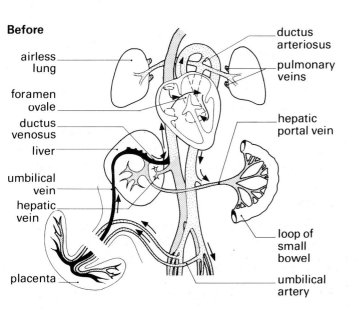

airless lung

foramen ovale

ductus venosus

liver

umbilical vein

hepatic vein

placenta

ductus arteriosus

pulmonary veins

hepatic portal vein

loop of small bowel

umbilical artery

Blood then flows into the right atrium but does not then go through the lungs. The lungs are collapsed and offer a high resistance to blood flow. As the heart contracts, the majority of the blood goes through a hole in the dividing septum called the **foramen ovale** into the left atrium. Any blood that does go through the pulmonary artery by-passes the lungs by going through the **ductus arteriosus** and into the aorta.

The aorta supplies the whole foetus. A branch of the **iliac arteries** (arteries that supply the legs) returns blood to the placenta via the umbilical artery where carbon dioxide and wastes are transferred to the maternal circulation.

At birth, constriction of the umbilical arteries and vein increases resistance to blood flow and the general blood pressure increases. At the same time, the lungs fill with air, expand, and resistance to blood flow drops. Blood flows through the lungs and into the left atrium. This increase in pressure closes the foramen ovale so increasing blood flow to the lungs.

Constriction of the ductus venosus and ductus arteriosus completes the change to the 'normal' double circulation of the adult.

*SAQ 85* Will the percentage oxygen in the foetal blood at the following places be relatively high or low?
(*a*) Umbilical vein.
(*b*) Umbilical artery.
(*c*) Right atrium.
(*d*) Pulmonary artery.

*SAQ 86* Given that there is a mixing of oxygenated and deoxygenated foetal blood, how is it that enough oxygen can be supplied for development to continue? (Mixing of blood is fatal in adults!)

*SAQ 87* How will the composition of blood change in the right atrium and pulmonary artery after birth?

## 4.15 *Extension:* Birth control and family planning

Human beings now understand a great deal about the process of conception that results in the birth of a new individual. In the light of this knowledge, many differing methods have been developed to ensure that the act of coitus need not be followed by the implantation and development of an embryo. This makes it possible for parents to have a definite choice about when or whether to start a family and the number of their children and the time gap between them.

AV 5 looks at various methods of birth control and considers their implications and use.

### AV 5: Birth control

**Materials**

VCR and monitor
ABAL video sequence — *Birth control*
worksheets 1 and 2

**Procedure**

(*a*) Check that you have all the relevant materials for this activity.
(*b*) Check that the video cassette is set up ready to show the appropriate sequence, *Birth control*.
(*c*) Start the VCR and stop it to complete the worksheets as indicated in the film.
(*d*) If you do not understand anything, stop the video, rewind, and study the relevant material again before consulting your tutor.
(*e*) If possible, work through the video and worksheets with a small group and discuss the material with your fellow students.

# Section 5 Sexual reproduction in angiosperms

## 5.1 Introduction and objectives

The reproductive organs of angiosperms are contained within the flowers. A flower consists of a series of modified leaves which form sepals, petals and the male and female organs.

The transfer of pollen from male organs to female organs is necessary before fertilisation can occur. In some flowers the pollen is dispersed by wind. This is a wasteful process and vast quantities of pollen must be produced.

However, many flowers are brightly coloured, scented and produce nectar. These adaptations attract insects which act as very efficient pollinators for the majority of flowers.

This section studies the structure of flowers, pollination and subsequent fertilisation. It then considers the development of fruits and the embryo that forms within. Finally, the similarities and differences of reproduction in angiosperms and mammals are investigated.

After working through this section you should be able to do the following:
(a) Investigate the structure of flowers.
(b) Describe the structure of a generalised flower.
(c) Define cross-pollination and self-pollination.
(d) Give an account of:
    (i) mechanisms which promote cross-pollination;
    (ii) the characteristics of insect and wind-pollinated flowers.
(e) Describe the development of the pollen tube.
(f) Describe:
    (i) double fertilisation in angiosperms;
    (ii) the development of fruit and seed after fertilisation.
(g) Compare the methods of reproduction used by mammals and angiosperms.

## 5.2 The structure of flowers

A flower contains the angiosperm organs of sexual reproduction. It is considered to be formed from a modified shoot. The modified leaves of the shoot are arranged in concentric rings or **whorls** on the flower stalk or **receptacle,** as indicated in figure 79.

Figure 80 shows this same arrangement as it might exist in a longitudinal section through a typical dicotyledonous flower.

*SAQ 88* What structures make up the androecium?

**79  Diagrammatic plan of flower structure to show arrangement of whorls**

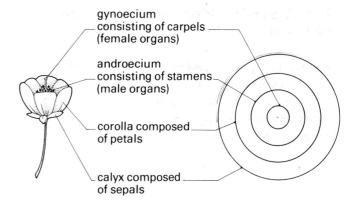

gynoecium
consisting of carpels
(female organs)

androecium
consisting of stamens
(male organs)

corolla composed
of petals

calyx composed
of sepals

**80  Longitudinal section through a generalised flower (dicot)**

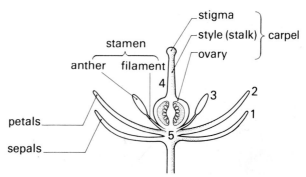

stigma
style (stalk) ⎱ carpel
stamen
ovary
anther    filament
4
petals
sepals
3    2
1
5

55

**81   Floral morphology of *Tulipa* (the tulip)**

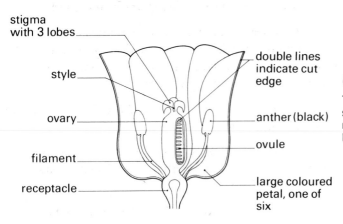

stigma with 3 lobes

style

ovary

filament

receptacle

double lines indicate cut edge

anther (black)

ovule

large coloured petal, one of six

(a) **Half flower drawing**

The flower is cut into two equal parts longitudinally with a sharp instrument. One half is then drawn *accurately* in 3D making *double* lines where parts are cut. All parts are clearly labelled

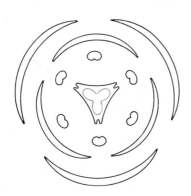

(b) **Floral diagram**

This is a transverse plan of the flower parts. It is *not* labelled.

(i) If sepals and petals are different, this should be indicated, e.g. ⌒ and ⌒

(ii) Parts that are linked together are shown by drawing relevant parts touching

(iii) Indicate whether stamens are attached to petals or free ⌣⌣ and whether they dehisce internally ⌒ or externally ⌣

(iv) Gynoecium – the style and stigma are not drawn. The ovary is shown in cross-section

(c) **Floral formula**

This gives details of the components of each whorl

Abbreviations for the whorls are as follows:

K = calyx
C = corolla
P = perianth. Used when calyx and corolla cannot be distinguished
A = androecium
G = gynoecium

$\overline{G}$ indicates that the ovary is inserted on the receptacle at a point beneath the insertion of the petals (inferior ovary)
$\underline{G}$ indicates that the ovary is inserted on the receptacle at a point above the insertion of the petals (superior ovary)
( ) indicates parts of a whorl are joined
$\overset{\frown}{C\ A}$ indicates components of 2 whorls, e.g. C and A, are joined

∞ = numerous

The floral formula for the tulip is $P_{3+3}$ $A_{3+3}$ $\underline{G}_3$

*SAQ 89* What structures make up the gynoecium?

*SAQ 90* What structure is identified as 5?

---

## Practical J: Investigating flower structure

In order to investigate the structure of a flower, it is necessary to examine each of its component parts. This means that each part of the specimen must be separated out and examined with a hand lens or a binocular microscope.

Observations are usually recorded as (*a*) half flower drawing, (*b*) floral diagram, (*c*) floral formula.

Figure 81 shows each of these (a–c) for a tulip.

### Materials

flowers (as available by season — select contrasting types), razor blade, white tile, slides, coverslips, binocular microscope or hand lens, fine forceps.

### Procedure

(*a*) Select one flower and identify each of the whorls on your specimen. You may have to pull the petals back or remove them to see the stamens and gynoecium in the centre of the flower. Keep any parts you remove for procedure point (*c*).
(*b*) Select two different flowers and investigate the structure of each. Record your observations as shown in figure 81(a) in your practical notebook.
(*c*) Work out the floral formula and floral diagram for *one* flower.

(The petals of many flowers are brightly coloured and some also have nectaries, which produce nectar, a sugary secretion. Some flowers also have coloured stripes, long rows of hairs and attractive scents. Indicate features such as these on your half flower diagram.)

Show this work to your tutor.

Some flowers, e.g. the tulip, are radially symmetrical. Their petals are all similar. Such flowers are described as being **actinomorphic.**

Other flowers, e.g. snapdragon (*Antirrhinum*) and dead nettle (*Lamium*) are bilaterally symmetrical. The petals are not all the same size and shape. These flowers are called **zygomorphic.**

The petals of a tulip are free and the flower is said to be **polypetalous.**

The petals of *Antirrhinum* and *Lamium* are partly joined to form a tube. This type of flower is said to be **sympetalous.**

The gynoecium is formed from one or more carpel. A carpel may be thought of as a leaf-like structure which bears ovules along its edges. However, this structure enfolds itself so that the ovules come to lie in vertical rows inside the cavity (locule) thus formed (see figure 82).

### 82   A generalised carpel

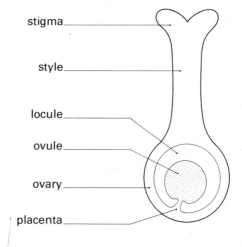

A simple gynoecium is composed of a single carpel divided into three regions, stigma, style and ovary. Several carpels are often produced by a single flower. Each carpel may be separate or, more usually, they are fused together. Figure 83 shows a TS through the ovary of a gynoecium formed from three carpels, containing six rows of ovules.

Each ovule contains an egg cell or female gamete which is inside a structure called the embryo sac — see figure 84. Notice that the embryo sac has eight nuclei.

**83    TS of an ovary**

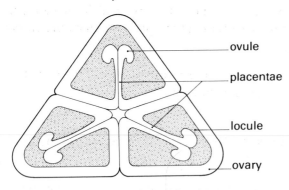

- ovule
- placentae
- locule
- ovary

**84    Vertical section through a generalised ovule**

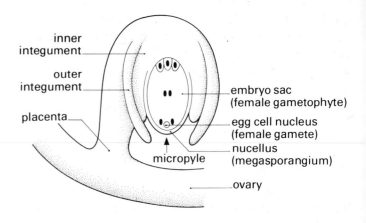

- inner integument
- outer integument
- placenta
- embryo sac (female gametophyte)
- egg cell nucleus (female gamete)
- nucellus (megasporangium)
- micropyle
- ovary

The androecium is made up of the stamens. A typical stamen is composed of a stalk or filament and a two-lobed anther. The important function of the stamen is to produce the microspore mother cells which give rise to the pollen grains containing the male gametes. The cross-section of the anther (figure 85) shows where the pollen is produced. Each anther lobe is divided into two pollen sacs.

When ripe, part of the anther wall becomes lignified and splits open (dehisces) as it dries, thus releasing pollen. Pollen may remain loosely attached to the dehisced wall.

**85    TS of an anther**

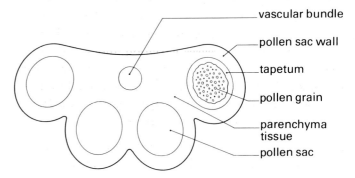

- vascular bundle
- pollen sac wall
- tapetum
- pollen grain
- parenchyma tissue
- pollen sac

## Practical K: Examination of carpels, anthers and pollen grains

### Materials

flowers (as available by season), razor blade, white tile for cutting on, slides, coverslips, binocular microscope or hand lens, dilute detergent or alcohol.

### Procedure

(a) Remove the sepals, petals and anthers which surround the gynoecium in one flower. Examine the gynoecium with a hand lens, identifying the stigma, style and ovary.

In some flowers, the petals, sepals and stamens may have withered, leaving only the carpels. What has happened to the ovary in these flowers?

(b) Examine the internal structure of the gynoecium by cutting one transversely and another longitudinally. Make a labelled drawing of the ovary to show the arrangement of the ovules within the ovary. Figures 82 and 83 should help you with this.
(c) Unripe anthers have no pollen attached to the outside. Dissect out an unripe anther and cut across it transversely.
(d) Examine it with a hand lens, noting the four pollen sacs, which are packed with pollen — see figure 85.
(e) Ripe anthers have pollen grains on the outside. Dissect out a ripe anther and cut across it transversely.
(f) Examine it with a hand lens and make a quick drawing to show how the anther has burst open to

release the ripe pollen.

(g) Shake some pollen on to a microscope slide, mount it in a drop of dilute detergent or alcohol and note its appearance under both high and lower power. Draw a few pollen grains from different flowers. Flowers can be identified on the basis of their pollen grains which are very distinctive.

Show this work to your tutor.

## 5.3 Pollination

The transfer of pollen from an anther to a stigma is called pollination. Transfer of pollen may involve either cross-pollination, or self-pollination.

**Cross-pollination.** Pollen is transferred from the anther on one flower to the stigma of a flower of another plant. Most flowers normally cross-pollinate. Cross-pollination increases variation and a number of mechanisms have evolved which improve the chances of cross-pollination. Pollination can be brought about by insects or by wind. Other agents such as birds, bats and water are used by some flowers.

Insect-pollinated flowers are called **entomophilous** (insect-loving) flowers; wind-pollinated flowers are called **anemophilous** (wind-loving) flowers.

**Self-pollination.** Pollen is transferred from the anther to the stamen of a flower of the same plant. This occurs commonly in plants such as the garden pea.

The following is a list of mechanisms which help to ensure cross-pollination.

**Protandry** (Greek: *proto,* first; *andros,* male). The stamens ripen before the carpels, e.g. ivy, geranium.

**Protogyny** (Greek; *proto,* first; *gyne,* female). The carpels ripen before the stamens, e.g. wild arum.

Unisexual flowers are produced, which show either the **monoecious** condition — the male and female flowers are on the same plant, e.g. hazel, beech, ash, or the **dioecious** condition — the male and female flowers are on separate plants, e.g. holly, willow, poplar.

**Self-sterility.** In some plants, pollen will not develop on stigmas of the same plant, for example, in some orchids, some apple varieties and red clover.

(These mechanisms are studied more fully in the unit *Genetics.*)

**86    Differences between anemophilous and entomophilous flowers**

| Characteristic | Insect-pollinated flowers | Wind-pollinated flowers |
|---|---|---|
| (1) *Petals* | | |
| (a) Are they large and brightly coloured? | | |
| (b) Do they have nectaries, | | |
| (c) and/or scent? | | |
| (d) Do they form a landing platform or make it easy for insects to alight on the flower? | | |
| (2) *Anthers* | | |
| (a) Are they large? | | |
| (b) Are they loosely attached to the filament? | | |
| (c) Do they hang outside the flower or are they inside the flower? | | |
| (d) Is the pollen powdery or does it form clumps? | | |
| (e) Is the pollen smooth-surfaced or rough? | | |
| (3) *Stigma* | | |
| (a) Is the stigma feathery or flat, lobed and sticky? | | |
| (b) Does the stigma hang outside the flower or is it inside the flower? | | |

## Practical L: Characteristics of insect and wind-pollinated flowers

### Materials

insect and wind-pollinated flowers, hand lens

### Procedure

(*a*) Examine the flowers provided.
Summarise the structural differences between anemophilous and entomophilous flowers by copying the table in figure 86 into your notebook and completing it.
(*b*) How do the characteristics (1) to (3) aid in wind-pollination? Explain this briefly but clearly in your notebook.

Show this work to your tutor.

### 5.3.1 Extension: The evolution of flowers and insects

EITHER obtain the book *Life on Earth* by David Attenborough (published by Collins/BBC or Fontana). In Chapter 3 'The first forests' read from page 80, mid-page 'Plants now began to turn the flying skills of insects to their own advantage ...' up to the end of the chapter. Make brief notes on the main adaptations discussed.

OR read Scientific American Offprint No. 12. *The Fertilisation of Flowers* by Verne Grant (Vol. 184, No. 6, June 1951, pp. 52–56). Make brief notes on the main adaptations of flowers to their pollinating agents.

## 5.4 The gametes of angiosperms

The flowering plant body is diploid. Meiosis occurs in the flower within the anthers and the ovules.

Gametogenesis in angiosperms was studied briefly in section 3.4 of this unit. Study figure 39 once more. Look first at the production of the female gamete. This occurs within the ovule. The embryo sac, which includes the female gamete, develops from a single diploid cell, the megaspore mother cell. Figure 87

shows the development of the embryo sac.

The male gamete develops within each pollen grain, which forms within the anther (Again see figure 39.) The pollen sac wall produces diploid pollen mother cells. Figure 88 shows the development of a pollen grain.

After pollination, the generative nucleus divides mitotically giving rise to two male gametes.

**87 Development of the embryo sac containing the female gamete**

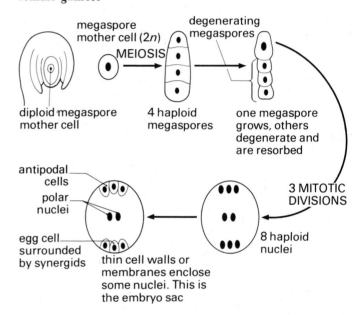

**88 Development of a pollen grain**

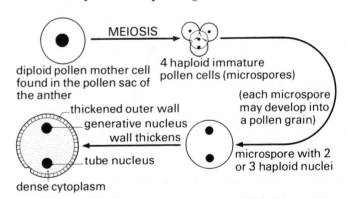

## 5.5 The development of the pollen tube and fertilisation

As a result of pollination, pollen grains are

## 89 The development of the pollen tube

(i) Pollen grain on sticky surface of stigma

style

(ii) The pollen tube grows out of the pollen grain and down through the style and ovary wall. It literally 'eats' its way through the tissues secreting digestive enzymes at its tip. The tube nucleus is in the tip of the pollen tube, the generative nucleus follows behind

polar nuclei

(iii) The generative nucleus divides mitotically to form 2 male gametes which move down the pollen tube and eventually fuse with the polar nuclei and the egg nucleus

Synergid may guide male gametes

egg nucleus

micropyle

(iv) Tube nucleus remains in the tip of the pollen tube as it grows

(v) When the embryo sac has been penetrated by the tube nucleus, the nucleus disintegrates and leaves a clear way for the two male nuclei to follow. One male nucleus fuses with the female gamete, the egg nucleus, and this results in a diploid zygote which will develop into a new plant. The other male nucleus fuses with the two polar nuclei and this results in a triploid nucleus which develops into the endosperm. This sequence of events is known as double fertilisation and is unique to the angiosperms

transferred on to the sticky stigma surface. In order to reach the ovule, the male gametes have to travel down the length of the style and penetrate the ovary wall. This is achieved by means of the pollen tube which grows out of the pollen grain into the tissues of the style. The process is summarised in figure 89.

---

## Practical M: Observing pollen-tube formation

In many plants, the stigma and style tissues contain sugar, which appears to be essential for pollen germination. The aim of this practical is to observe pollen-tube formation.

### Materials

chinagraph pencil, pollen from two or three flowers, cavity slides, coverslips, paint brush, needle, Pasteur pipettes, $0.4$ mol $dm^{-3}$ sucrose solution, distilled water, neutral red or acetocarmine stain, access to incubator, if possible

### Procedure

(a) Place a drop of sucrose solution in one of the cavity slides. Label the slide 'sucrose'.
(b) Using a paint brush, transfer some pollen from the flowers provided into the drop of sucrose solution. Cover with a coverslip.
(c) Repeat the procedure, substituting distilled water for sucrose.
(d) Place both preparations in a dark place, preferably in an incubator at about 30 °C, and examine at twenty-minute intervals over the next two to three hours.
(e) When the pollen grains have germinated, irrigate the slides with neutral red or acetocarmine. Look for the tube nucleus and the two male nuclei.
(f) Make annotated diagrams of your observations.

### Extension

(g) How would you investigate the effects of the following variables on the germination of pollen grains:
(i) sugar concentration;
(ii) temperature?

Describe, with full experimental details, how you would carry out this investigation.

Show this work to your tutor.

---

## AV 6 Growth of pollen tubes

This short sequence shows the growth of a pollen tube and provides and alternative (or addition) to practical M.

## Materials

VCR and monitor
ABAL video sequence — *Growth of pollen tubes*
figure 89 from student's guide
worksheet

## Procedure

(*a*) Check that you have all the relevant materials for this activity.

(*b*) Check that the video cassette is set up ready to show the appropriate sequence, *Growth of pollen tubes*.

(*c*) Start the VCR and view the sequence. Study figure 89 in the student's guide again. View the sequence for a second time.

(*d*) Complete the worksheet. If you do not understand anything, stop the video, rewind, and study the relevant material again before consulting your tutor.

(*e*) If possible, work through the video and worksheet with a small group and discuss the material with your fellow students.

## 5.6 Development of seed and fruit

Following fertilisation, (*a*) the ovule develops into the seed, (*b*) the zygote divides and differentiates into the embryo, (*c*) the endosperm nucleus divides to form nutritive tissue, (*d*) the integuments become the testa, (*e*) the ovary wall becomes the fruit. Figure 90 summarises the development of a fertilised ovule.

The cotyledons may develop and fill the entire embryo sac replacing the endosperm as the nutrient source. This happens, for example, in the broad bean. The structure of this seed will be investigated in section 7. In a seed like castor oil, much of the endosperm remains.

While the seed is developing, the ovary wall is growing to allow the expansion of the seeds. The ovary wall becomes the pericarp and the outer layer of this forms the 'skin' of the fruit. The fruit plays an important part in the dispersal of the seed within.

It may
— develop into a fleshy food source for animals, e.g. raspberry

### 90 The development of the ovule after fertilisation of the egg nucleus

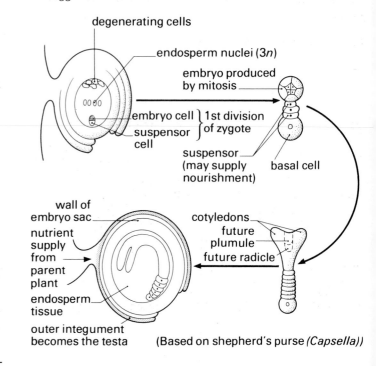

(Based on shepherd's purse *(Capsella)*)

— dry to form a dehiscing mechanism, e.g. gorse
— acquire wings or hooks for wind or animal dispersal, e.g. sycamore or goose-grass.
— develop layers as in the plum where the outer skin attracts by colour, middle forms food 'bait' and inner layer forms the woody protective stone.

Figure 91 shows the fruit produced by *Capsella*

Hormones coordinate the development of the seed and fruit. Fruit ripening is also under hormonal control.

## 5.7 Summary assignment 8

The following question is taken from a Southern Universities Joint Board Examination in 1977.

Describe the flower of a *named* angiosperm. Explain how its structures produce gametes, ensure cross-fertilisation and provide for the developing zygote.

Prepare an answer to this question in the form of concise notes and diagrams.

Remember that where a diagram provides information, there is no need to repeat this in written notes.

Show this work to your tutor.

**91 Fruit of *Capsella* (shepherd's purse)**

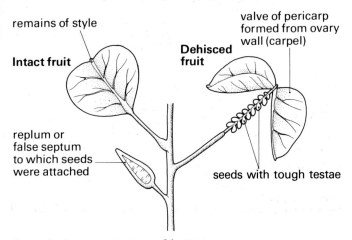

remains of style

**Intact fruit**

valve of pericarp formed from ovary wall (carpel)

**Dehisced fruit**

replum or false septum to which seeds were attached

seeds with tough testae

*Capsella* develops the type of fruit known as a capsule which dries to form a dehiscing mechanism

## 5.8 Comparison of sexual reproduction in mammals and flowering plants

Making a comparison always involves looking for both differences and similarities. On the basis of answers to the following questions, draw up *either* a table of comparison *or* a list of points arranged under the headings 'similarities' and 'differences'. You may think of other points for comparison in addition to these.

1 Parents (are they monoecious or dioecious?)
2 Reproductive structures (permanent or temporary — mobile or stationary?)
3 Gametes (isogametes or heterogametes — method of transfer — is male gamete active or inactive?)
4 Fertilisation (internal or external?)
5 Embryonic development (internal or external — food supply — protection — continuous or interrupted?)
6 Offspring (potential numbers — survival rate — dispersal methods — food and protection after separation from parent — like or unlike parent?)

Show this work to your tutor.

Self test 6, page 110, covers section 5 of this unit.

# Section 6 The role of water in sexual reproduction

## 6.1 Introduction and objectives

Many aquatic organisms release their gametes into the surrounding water and it is here that fertilisation and development of the zygote occur. (Whenever gametes are released outside an organism into the environment, fertilisation is said to be external.)

Environmental water plays a vital role in the reproductive process and has three main functions:
(*a*) it prevents desiccation (drying out) of the gametes. Once the gametes have been released from a parent, they would soon dry up unless surrounded by water;
(*b*) it enables sperm to move. Sperm are able to swim through the water to fertilise eggs;
(*c*) it provides a medium in which the embryos can develop. It prevents their desiccation, contains dissolved oxygen and facilitates the removal of waste materials.

Sexually reproducing terrestrial organisms such as mammals and flowering plants, do not need external environmental water for reproduction. However, it is believed that terrestrial organisms evolved from aquatic ancestors. During this evolution, mechanisms were acquired which enabled them to reproduce without the need for an external watery environment.

There are, however, some organisms which are able to live on land but which, nevertheless, need external water for reproduction. Examples include frogs, mosses and ferns. These organisms represent a 'half-way house' between the aquatic mode of life and the truly terrestrial one. They have many structural and physiological features in common with land organisms, but their reproduction is geared to an aquatic environment. Amphibians, like the common frog, migrate to water in order to breed. Mosses and ferns, without being actually aquatic, require at least a film of water for the male gametes to swim through, and thus can only reproduce successfully in damp habitats.

During reproduction in most land organisms, neither the gametes or the embryos are ever exposed directly to the drying effects of the atmosphere. They are kept in a watery medium inside the reproductive organs or other special structures. Sperm are transferred from the male organs to the female organs, fertilisation occurring within the female's body (internal fertilisation). The female reproductive organs provide a watery medium in which the embryo develops.

In some organisms, the zygote is retained within the female and is protected during its development into an embryo, as in mammals and flowering plants. Animals which bear live young are described as **viviparous.** In other organisms, such as insects and birds, the embryo develops outside the female, but is always surrounded by a protective coat or a shell which encloses a watery medium. Animals which lay eggs are called **oviparous.**

After working through this section you should be able to do the following:
(*a*) Describe the role of water in sexual reproduction for (i) fertilisation, (ii) development of embryo, (iii) release of spores.
(*b*) Explain how terrestrial organisms can reproduce sexually without the need for environmental water.
(*c*) Describe mechanisms which increase the chances of successful fertilisation.
(*d*) Describe and compare sexual reproduction in *Spirogyra, Fucus, Hydra,* herring, frog, dogfish, moss and fern.

## 6.2 Reproduction in an aquatic environment

In this section you will be asked to refer to other books for information on reproduction in named organisms. Your tutor will give you a reference list. Many marine invertebrates, e.g. ragworms, simply release egg and sperm into the water where external fertilisation occurs. Such a release of gametes is coordinated, usually as a response to day length, the phases of the moon or water temperature. Behavioural changes in the spawning period may result in large numbers of mature organisms gathering in one area so that the chances of fertilisation of eggs are increased.

However, some simple invertebrate animals such as *Hydra* show a pattern of sexual reproduction which is a little different from this.

Consult a zoology or biology reference book giving an account of sexual reproduction in *Hydra,* and answer the following questions.

**SAQ 91** Which cells of the body wall give rise to the gonads?

**SAQ 92** What separates the oocyte from the surrounding water?

**SAQ 93** Some species of *Hydra* are hermaphrodite. How is cross-fertilisation encouraged?

**SAQ 94** How is the pattern of fertilisation in *Hydra* different from the generalised account of aquatic invertebrate reproduction in the introduction to this sub-section?

**SAQ 95** When the pond water becomes stagnant, *Hydra* is stimulated to reproduce sexually. How does this enhance the survival of the species under unfavourable conditions?

For most of the year, herring swim in shoals in offshore waters. In the breeding season, they move inshore to spawning grounds in the estuaries of rivers. In the spawning grounds, the males and females congregate. When a female releases her eggs, a nearby male immediately releases sperm over them.

Each female herring can release 50,000 eggs at a time, but this is a small number compared with some other female fish, e.g. cod, which can release up to seven million at a time!

Fertilised herring eggs sink and become attached to gravel or seaweed. The tiny fish which hatch from herring eggs are planktonic (drifting in the surface waters) and many are eaten by other animals.

**SAQ 96** Consult a reference book and read how a dogfish reproduces. Do not worry about details of its reproductive system. Draw up a table to compare reproduction in a dogfish with the account of reproduction in the herring given previously.

Consult a reference book for details of mating in frogs and toads and answer the following questions:

**SAQ 97** What are the advantages of a breeding season in frogs?

**SAQ 98** State the advantages of courtship behaviour as shown by frogs;

**SAQ 99** State how fertilisation in a frog (*a*) differs from and (*b*) is similar to, fertilisation in a herring.

**SAQ 100** What are the functions of the jelly-coat surrounding the eggs of frogs?

*Spirogyra* is a fresh-water green, filamentous alga. Sexual reproduction follows a pattern know as conjugation. Study figure 92 and read about this process for yourself and answer the questions. (Remember that the cells of a *Spirogyra* filament are haploid.)

**SAQ 101** How are gametes formed?

**SAQ 102** In what way could you distinguish between male and female gametes?

**SAQ 103** Is fertilisation external or internal?

**SAQ 104** Sexual reproduction usually occurs at the end of the growing season. Suggest a reason for this.

Figure 93 shows sexual reproduction in *Fucus serratus,* the Saw or Serrated Wrack, a brown seaweed found low down on the seashore. Many seaweeds reproduce in a similar manner.

filament of spirogyra cells

Conjugation tube forms between adjacent
cells of neighbouring filaments

Contents of one cell move through conjugation tube into adjacent cell.
The two nuclei fuse to form a zygote

Zygote develops thick protective wall and becomes a zygospore

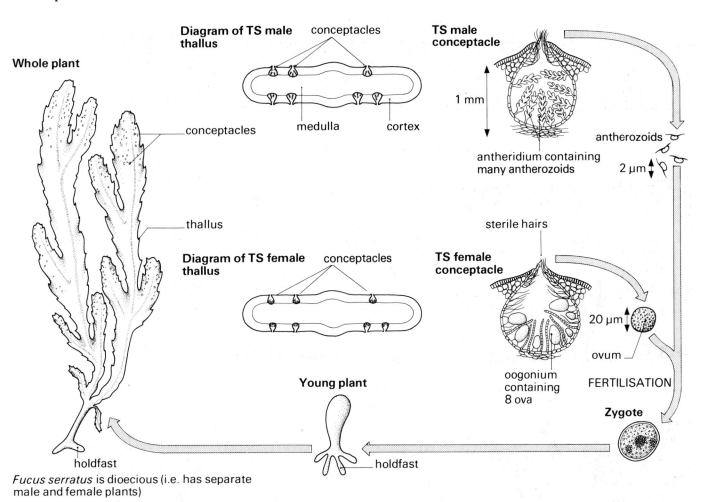

**Whole plant**

**Diagram of TS male thallus** — conceptacles

conceptacles

thallus

medulla   cortex

**TS male conceptacle**

1 mm

antheridium containing many antherozoids

antherozoids

2 μm

**Diagram of TS female thallus** — conceptacles

conceptacles

sterile hairs

**TS female conceptacle**

20 μm

ovum

oogonium containing 8 ova

FERTILISATION

**Young plant**

holdfast

holdfast

**Zygote**

*Fucus serratus* is dioecious (i.e. has separate male and female plants)

Read about reproduction in *Fucus serratus* and answer the following questions:

*SAQ 105* List three differences between the methods of reproduction by *Spirogyra* and *Fucus*.

*SAQ 106* How is the zygospore of *Spirogyra* different from the zygote of *Fucus*?

## 6.3 Reproduction in a terrestrial environment: mosses and ferns

Mosses and ferns probably evolved from aquatic algal-type ancestors which required environmental water for sexual reproduction. Although structures such as an impermeable epidermis and a vascular system have evolved which enable mosses and ferns to live on land, their reproduction is still dependent on environmental water. In both cases, this water acts as the medium through which the sperm move.

---

### Practical N: Reproduction in a moss

---

### The moss gametophyte

In mosses (and ferns) gamete production is carried out by a plant bearing sexual organs. These plants are called **gametophytes.** Figure 94 shows the

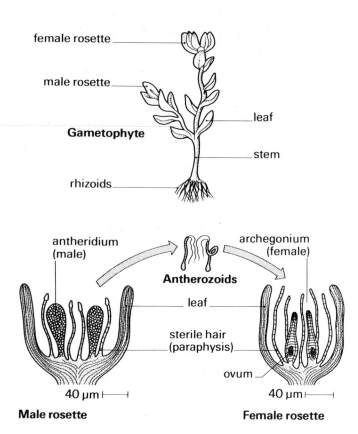

female rosette

male rosette

**Gametophyte**

leaf

stem

rhizoids

antheridium (male)

**Antherozoids**

archegonium (female)

leaf

sterile hair (paraphysis)

ovum

40 μm

40 μm

**Male rosette**

**Female rosette**

(b) Using the binocular microscope, look for the sex organs. The male organs are found in cup-like clusters of 'leaves' called **rosettes,** on slender side branches. The female rosettes are situated at the top of shoots in *Funaria.*

(c) Carefully remove a male rosette and tease out the contents in a drop of water on a slide and cover with coverslip. Examine under high power, noting the antheridia, **paraphyses** (hair-like structures) and sperm cells (**antherozoids**) — see figures 94 and 95. If possible, make a drawing of your preparation.

(d) Carefully remove a female rosette and tease out in a drop of water on a slide and cover with a coverslip. Examine under high power and identify the archegonia. If possible, make a drawing of your preparation. If your preparations were unsatisfactory, examine prepared vertical sections of male and female rosettes under low power. Make drawings of male and female rosettes.

### The moss sporophyte

After fertilisation, the zygote grows and develops into a spore-producing plant, or **sporophyte**, which remains attached to the female rosette of the gametophyte. The sporophyte is green but has no

**95  EM of male rosette**

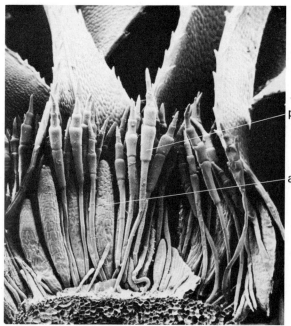

paraphysis

antheridium

gametophyte and sex organs of a moss, *Funaria*. The male sex organs are called **antheridia** and the female sex organs **archegonia.**

### Materials

Moss plant gametophyte, vertical section of male and female rosettes showing sex organs, binocular microscope, monocular microscope, slides, coverslips, needle

### Procedure

(a) Examine the moss plant gametophyte, noting the stem, 'leaves' and the root-like rhizoids. Mount a rhizoid and a 'leaf' in water and examine microscopically. Make an annotated drawing of your specimen.

leaves and depends largely, though not wholly, on the gametophyte for food. (See figure 96.)

**96   Sporophyte and gametophyte of *Funaria***

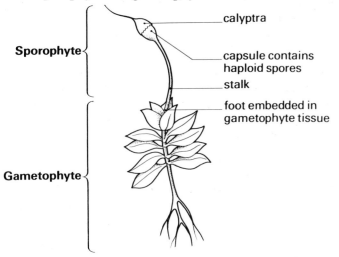

calyptra

capsule contains haploid spores

stalk

foot embedded in gametophyte tissue

## Materials

monocular and binocular microscopes, moss sporophyte, slides, coverslips, water, needles, Plasticine, slide of section of a sporophyte capsule

## Procedure

(*a*) Examine the sporophyte carefully, noting the spore capsule, stalk and foot. Make an annotated drawing of your specimen.
(*b*) Stick a small lump of Plasticine onto a slide. Remove an undehisced (unopened) capsule and gently push the remains of the stalk into the Plasticine with the capsule pointing up.
(*c*) Examine the preparation under a binocular microscope and carefully remove the hood-like covering, the **calyptra,** if present. The calyptra is derived from the gametophyte archegonium.
(*d*) Remove the lid or **operculum** of the capsule beneath which are the **peristomal teeth.** Breathe on the capsule for about fifteen seconds, and then observe the teeth again. Record your observations. (If nothing occurs, repeat with a dehisced (opened) capsule.) Figure 97 shows the peristomal teeth.
(*e*) Cut the spore capsule open and examine the spores.

(*f*) Examine a prepared slide of a section through a capsule. Note the spore sac, spores, annulus cells (the ring of cells where the operculum was joined to the capsule), teeth, operculum and photosynthetic tissue containing chloroplasts.

Under suitable conditions, the spores are released and germinate. Each spore is capable of developing into a gametophyte. (See figure 98.)
(*g*) Draw a section through a capsule to include all the structures mentioned in (*f*).

## Discussion of results

1 How does the structure of rhizoids and leaves of the gametophyte compare with roots and leaves of angiosperms?
2 The paraphyses are believed to hold water in the rosettes. Why is this necessary?
3 How is fertilisation brought about and where do you think the zygote develops?
4 Under what conditions do you think moss spores are released from the sporophyte capsule? Give reasons for your answers.
5 Figure 99 shows the life-cycle of *Funaria*. Copy the

**97   EM of peristomal teeth in *Funaria***

peristomal teeth

## 98   Germination of a moss spore

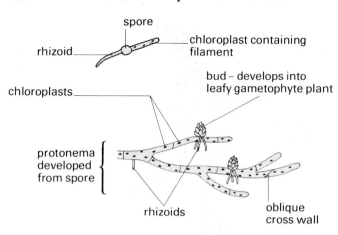

## 99   *Funaria* life-cycle

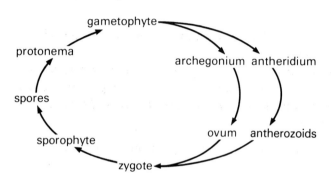

## 100   The gametophyte (prothallus) of *Dryopteris*

**Archegonium**

lower surface
of prothallus
cells of venter
ventral canal
nucleus
oosphere
neck cells
neck canal nuclei
cap cell

**Prothallus – ventral view**

rhizoids

**Antheridium**

2 ring cells
antherozoids
cap cell

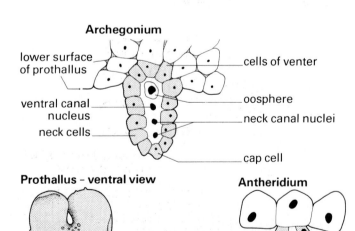

diagram and for each stage write a brief description of its structure, how it obtains food and its dependence on water or changes in humidity.

---

### Practical O: Reproduction in a fern

---

### The fern gametophyte

Figure 100 shows the gametophyte of a fern, *Dryopteris,* bearing sexual organs. Refer to this during your practical investigation. Notice that in ferns the gametophyte is a small heart-shaped structure called a **prothallus.** It lives independently of the large spore-producing plant (the sporophyte) with which you may be more familiar.

### Materials

monocular and binocular microscopes, fern prothallus (if available), slides, coverslips, needles, distilled water, prepared whole mounts of a prothallus and a section through a prothallus

### Procedure

(*a*) If available, carefully mount the gametophyte in water, lower surface uppermost. Examine it under both low and high power.
(*b*) Examine a prepared whole mount of a prothallus, using both low and high power.
Observe the antheridia (male sex organs) and the archegonia (female sex organs). Look for sperm and egg cells. Make a drawing of the prothallus to show the position of the archegonia and antheridia.
(*c*) Examine a prepared vertical section of a prothallus to observe antheridia and archegonia in side view. Make drawings of each.

### The fern sporophyte

The zygote develops eventually into a sporophyte. At first, this is small and dependent upon the small gametophyte for food. After its leaves and roots have developed, the sporophyte becomes independent of

**101  The young sporophyte of *Dryopteris***

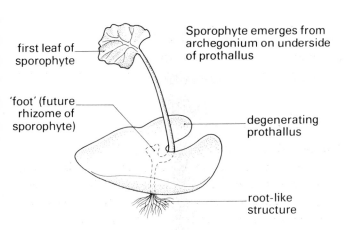

first leaf of sporophyte

Sporophyte emerges from archegonium on underside of prothallus

'foot' (future rhizome of sporophyte)

degenerating prothallus

root-like structure

**102  Mature sporophyte plant of *Dryopteris***

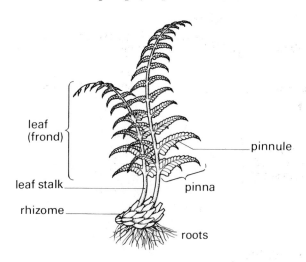

leaf (frond)

pinnule

leaf stalk

pinna

rhizome

roots

the gametophyte which withers and dies (see figures 101 and 102).

## Materials

monocular and binocular microscopes, slides, coverslips, slides of developing fern sporophytes, entire developed sporophtye with spores, slides of section through fern sporangia, Pasteur pipettes, concentrated glycerol, filter paper

## Procedure

(*a*) Examine slides of developing sporophytes, noting the leaves, the roots and the foot, which is embedded in the gametophyte.
(*b*) Examine an entire, mature sporophyte, noting the rhizome, leaf stalks and leaves (or **fronds**) which are sub-divided into **pinnae** and **pinnules** (see figure 102).
(*c*) Record your observations in the form of diagrams.

Some pinnules produce spores and are called **sporophylls** (spore-producing leaves). The spores are produced in **sporangia,** groups of which are found in structures called **sori** on the underside of the sporophylls. In some ferns, the sporangia are protected by an **indusium** (see figure 103).
(*d*) Remove a small section of a sporophyll and,

using a needle, prise an indusium away to reveal the sporangia.
(*e*) Mount some sporangia in a drop of water, cover with a coverslip and examine microscopically. Notice the spores, **stomium** and **annulus** cells. Make a drawing of your preparation.

Figures 104 and 105 show electron micrographs of fern sporangia.

**103  Sporophylls of *Dryopteris***

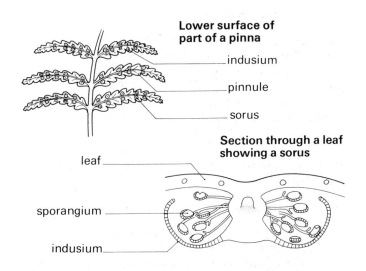

Lower surface of part of a pinna

indusium

pinnule

sorus

leaf

Section through a leaf showing a sorus

sporangium

indusium

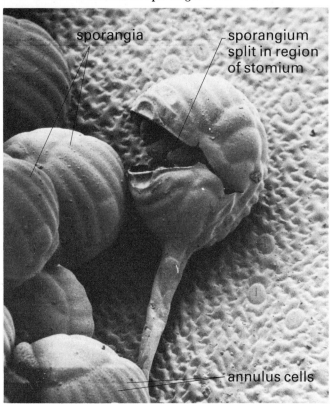

sporangia

sporangium
split in region
of stomium

annulus cells

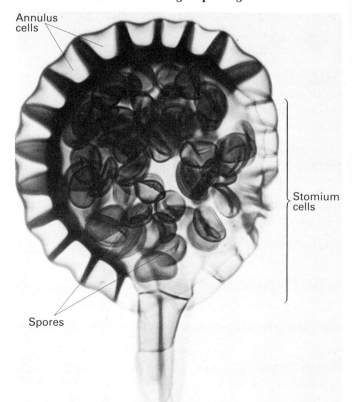

Annulus
cells

Stomium
cells

Spores

(*f*) While watching the sporangia under the microscope place a drop of concentrated glycerol at one edge of the coverslip and draw it through by means of a piece of filter paper at the opposite edge. Record any observations you make.

### Discussion of results

1 Under what conditions do you think sperms are released from the antheridia of the gametophyte? Explain your answer.
2 Where do you think the zygote develops?
3 Under what conditions do you think spores are released from the sporangium?
4 Describe the events in the fern life-cycle that require water or changing humidity.
5 Compare and contrast the reproduction and life-cycles of mosses and ferns.

The life-cycles of mosses and ferns include both a sexual, gamete-producing phase and an asexual, spore-producing phase. The sexual phase is always followed by the asexual phase, which is *always*

followed by another sexual phase, and so on. This regular alternation is called the **alternation of generations** and is typical of the life-cycle of all higher plants.

Alternation of generations is considered more fully in section 8 of this unit.

## 6.4 Conifers and flowering plants

You have already seen in section 5 that angiosperms, the flowering plants, achieve sexual reproduction in the terrestrial environment without the need for external sources of water other than those which keep the plant tissues in a turgid state.

Transfer of the male gamete to the female structure is achieved by means of pollination — either by wind or insects. Pollen itself has a thick, water-resistant wall to prevent desiccation.

Pollen grains on ripe stigmas of the correct species germinate and produce a pollen tube. Osmotic pressure is thought to enter into this process so moisture is essential for this stage. Germination of seeds (see section 7) is also dependent upon the availability of water.

**SAQ 107** From your study of reproduction in ferns and mosses (section 6.3):
(a) Which stage in the life-cycle is dependent on a water medium?
(b) What process is the water needed for?

The conifers and flowering plants show a reduction in the gametophyte generation which allows a greater independence from environmental water during reproduction.

**SAQ 108** What advantage does the greater independence from environmental water have for conifers and flowering plants?

The alternation of generations with reduced gametophyte stage is shown in figure 106.

Conifers produce pollen and seed-bearing cones on the one tree but on separate branches. Pollen production is copious for pollination depends upon wind. The female cone grows after pollination but fertilisation does not occur until the next year. Pollen

### 106 Alternation of generations in conifers and flowering plants

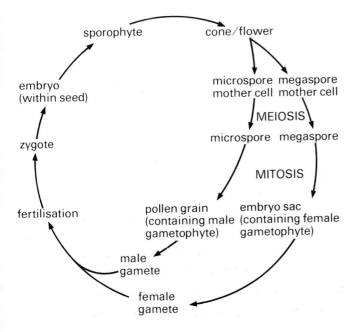

### 107 Reproduction in a conifer, *Pinus sylvestris*

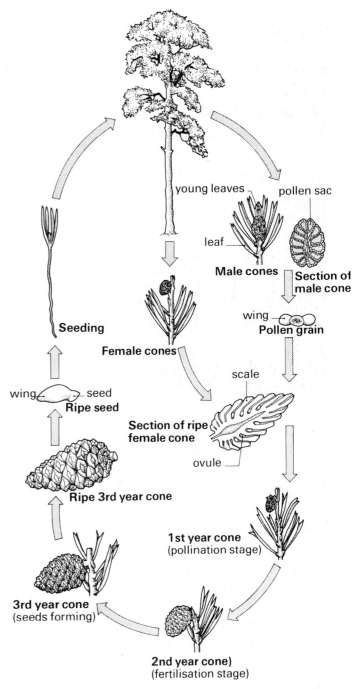

tubes are produced in a similar manner to angiosperms. The female cone ripens in the third year. At maturity, it is a dry brown woody structure with a pair of ripe seeds on the surface of each scale. As the cone dries, the scales of the cone separate and the liberated seeds are blown away by the wind.

## 6.5 Animal reproduction in a terrestrial environment

In all terrestrial animals, mechanisms have evolved which protect the gametes and the developing embryo from the drying effects of the atmosphere.

*SAQ 109* Sexual reproduction in the mammal was studied in section 4. Make a careful list of the ways in which mammals protect (*a*) gametes, (*b*) the developing embryo, from drying.

Insects have successfully exploited even the driest areas. The locust, for example, can breed in desert conditions. The male transfers sperm to the female by means of a penis. The sperm may be stored inside the female body, in a **spermatheca,** so eggs can be fertilised some time after mating has taken place.

The eggs are formed within egg tubes in the female's body. They receive a food store as they move down the tube. The 'shell' of the egg may be up to seven layers thick, perforated by micropyles through which a sperm can enter. After fertilisation, the eggs of some insects, e.g. the locust, are surrounded by an egg pod. The eggs of the cockroach are enclosed in a brown case of tanned protein.

Some female insects possess special **ovipositors** to place eggs under the surface of the soil, inside plant stems or even inside other insects.

The tough shells and internal membranes render insect eggs waterproof.

*SAQ 110* From this account, list the structures that enable an insect to protect (*a*) gametes, (*b*) the developing embryo, from drying.

Birds and reptiles produce large eggs within which the embryo develops surrounded by membranes, in particular, the amnion. Inside the amnion is the amniotic fluid which provides the embryo with an aquatic environment in which it can develop independently of an external source of water.

108   Section through a developing hen's egg

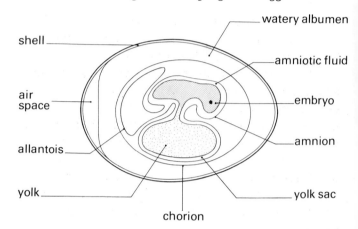

## 6.6 Summary assignment 9

1 Make a list of the various ways in which water is involved in reproductive processes. Provide an example of a named organism to illustrate each point.
2 Make a list of the adaptations of terrestrial organisms for reproduction in the absence of environmental water. Again, provide a named example for each adaptation.

Self test 7, page 110, covers section 6 of this unit.

# Section 7 Germination and development in dicotyledonous plants

## 7.1 Introduction and objectives

Section 5.6 described the first stage in the growth and development of a dicotyledonous plant, the formation of the embryo within a seed. When suitable conditions exist, this embryo will grow out of its protective seed case, a process called **germination,** and develop into a mature plant. During development the types of tissue found in the mature plant will differentiate from the meristems. As some types of plant develop, secondary growth, which results in a thickening of the plant, may occur and wood cells are differentiated. These stages of growth and development are examined in this section.

After working through this section, you should be able to do the following:
(*a*) Describe the structure and function of a dicotyledonous seed.
(*b*) List the conditions necessary for germination to occur and the stages involved in the two types of germination — epigeal and hypogeal.
(*c*) Give an account of the biochemical activities concerned with germination.
(*d*) Describe the structure and activity of apical meristems in dicotyledons and the differentiation of their derivative tissues including:
epidermis, collenchyma, parenchyma, sclerenchyma. phloem, cambium and xylem.
(*e*) Recognise and draw typical cells from the tissues listed in (*d*) above from transverse or longitudinal sections of the stem or root.
(*f*) Define what is meant by secondary growth.
(*g*) Explain how secondary growth arises from lateral meristems.
(*h*) Describe the results of secondary growth in herbaceous and woody dicotyledons.
(*i*) Describe the formation of cork.
(*j*) Identify secondary growth tissues and cells from transverse sections.

## 7.2 Seeds and germination

When liberated from the parent plant, seeds are usually in a resting or dormant condition. The following practicals investigate the structure and function of seeds and their pattern of germination.

---

### Practical P: Investigating the structure and function of a seed

---

☠ **Warning: Castor oil seeds contain poisonous substances.**

### Materials

6 broad beans (pre-soaked for 24 hours), blotting paper, 4 pins (entomological pins are best), glass dish with loosely fitting lid (see figure 112), polystyrene block (see figure 112), tile, iodine in KI, Benedict's solution, sodium hydroxide solution, copper sulphate solution, Sudan III, dropper, test tubes, beakers, Bunsen burner, seeds of castor oil, sunflower, pea and others.

### Procedure

(*a*) Examine a broad bean seed and identify the testa, micropyle and hilum (see figure 109).

### 109  Broad bean seed

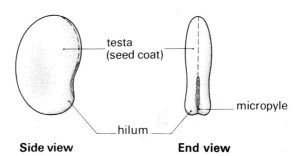

Side view          End view

75

(*b*) Remove the testa, as follows:

(i) hold the seed in the left hand with the hilum to the left;

(ii) run the thumbnail of the right hand down edge of the seed;

(iii) peel the testa off, holding the cotyledons firmly together.

(*c*) Carefully prise the cotyledons apart from the side opposite to the hilum so that the central part of the embryo is attached to one of them. Discard the other cotyledon.

(*d*) Identify the structures displayed in figure 110. Repeat stages (*b*) and (*c*) with four more broad bean seeds.

(*e*) Leave one of the cotyledons and its embryo intact and treat the other three as follows. Place the cotyledons on a tile and for one, cut away three-quarters of the cotyledon (figure 111).

For the second cut away all the cotyledon except for a small area beneath the plumule (see figure 111).

For the third, push a pin into the embryo at the point where the discarded cotyledon was attached to it and, keeping the embryo on the pin, prise it free from the cotyledon.

(*f*) Pin each of the portions of bean seed to the polystyrene block with the embryos towards the blotting paper and the radicles pointing downwards (see figure 112). When the pin is securely in the block, withdraw it about 1 mm to leave the embryo just clear of the blotting paper.

(*g*) Moisten the blotting paper and put the block into the glass dish. Add about 10 cm³ water and replace

**110   Seed of broad bean with testa and one cotyledon removed**

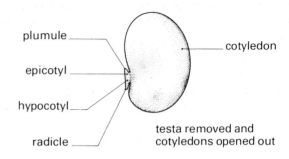

**111   Embryo with varying amounts of cotyledon attached**

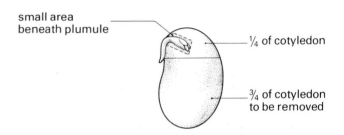

the lid loosely. Leave the dish in moderate light (not direct sunlight) for a week.

(*h*) After a week, remove the polystyrene block and the seedlings and measure the length of radicle and epicotyl and the number of lateral roots.

(*i*) Collate the results from your class and calculate the mean results before recording them in a suitable table of results.

**112   Dish containing embryos**

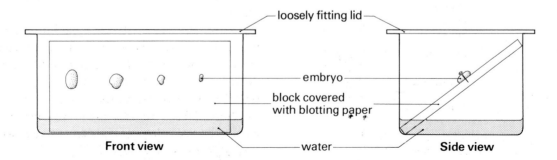

(*j*) Use remaining broad bean seed and test for presence of starch, sugars, protein and lipids or oils. (Lipids produce a red stain with Sudan III.) Use a dropper to treat cut surfaces of the seed with reagent.
(*k*) Record your findings from the food tests in the form of a table (see figure 113).
(*l*) Examine a castor oil seed. Figure 114 shows the external features which you should identify.
(*m*) Cut two seeds in half (i) down the flattened side, (ii) down the narrow side. Figure 114 shows the features which you should identify.
(*n*) Test for food reserves present in castor oil seed.
(*o*) Cut up and examine the other seeds provided. Food tests are not required for these seeds.

### Discussion of results

1 What part do cotyledons play in germination and early growth? Justify your answer with evidence from your results.
2 A broad bean seed is described as being a non-endospermic seed but the castor oil is an endospermic seed. What differences did you detect in structure and food reserves between these two seeds? Decide which of the other seeds you examined were endospermic and which were non-endospemic.

Show this work to your tutor.

**114   External and internal structure of castor oil seed (*Ricinus* sp.)**

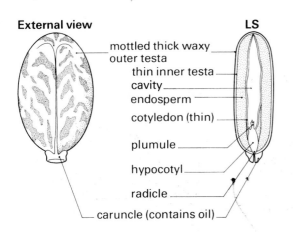

### 113   Table of results

| Name of seed | Food reserves present | | | |
| --- | --- | --- | --- | --- |
| | Starch | Reducing sugar | Protein | Lipid |
| | | | | |
| | | | | |

---

**Practical Q: Observing early growth and development**

---

### Introduction

In this practical you will be observing the external morphological changes which occur in the development of broad bean and castor oil plants from the seed stage. You will also be measuring their growth using increase in length as one criterion.

This will be a class practical. The work should be shared out among your class and observations and measurements collated at the end.

### Materials

20 seeds each of broad bean and castor oil, 2 × 250 cm³ beakers, 2 seed-trays with soil, marking pencil, balance for weighing, absorbent paper, fine sandpaper

### Procedure

(*a*) Weigh twenty seeds of broad bean and twenty seeds of castor oil. Record the total mass of both types of seed.
(*b*) Put twenty seeds of each type into separate labelled beakers. Add water to fill the beaker. Mark the uppermost level of the seeds on the side of the beaker. Leave for twenty-four hours.
(*c*) After twenty-four hours, examine each beaker carefully. Observe and record any changes which have occurred. Comparing soaked seeds with unsoaked ones may help.

(*d*) Remove the seeds from the beaker and blot with absorbent paper to remove excess moisture. Reweigh each group of seeds and record their mass. Calculate the percentage increase of mass for each group of seeds. If castor oil seeds do not appear to have taken up much water, rub the testa with sandpaper before planting.

(*e*) Label one seed-tray 'broad bean' and plant all twenty seeds of this type. Label the second tray 'castor oil' and plant these seeds. The seeds should be spaced out and buried underneath a 1 cm layer of damp soil. Keep in a warm place.

Observe and record changes in morphology and height, each day if possible, for ten days. (Check that soil remains moist.)

Record your observations of morphological changes in the form of annotated drawings which summarise the main changes and when they were observed.

(*f*) Record your class results for the height measurements in a suitable results table.

Draw a graph of your results.

### Discussion of results

There are two distinct types of germination known as hypogeal germination and epigeal germination. In **epigeal germination,** the hypocotyl elongates, rises above the soil surface and pulls the cotyledons above ground. The shoot system develops from the plumule but the cotyledons turn green and form the first leaves.

In **hypogeal germination,** it is the epicotyl which elongates, pushing the plumule above ground and leaving the cotyledons beneath the soil surface.

1 What changes occurred after seeds were soaked for twenty-four hours? Explain the causes and effects of these changes.
2 Which seeds show epigeal germination and which show hypogeal germination?
3 How is the delicate plumule protected in each type of seed as it breaks through the soil?
4 In epigeal germination, how do the cotyledons compare in appearance with the first foliage leaves?

5 What additional function is served by the cotyledons in plants that germinate in epigeal manner?
6 From your observations of morphological changes in the shoot during germination, suggest any criteria that you consider would give a useful picture of growth in the seedling.
7 Which seeds grow most rapidly during germination?

Show this work to your tutor.

## 7.3 Dormancy and germination

The embryo of a developing seed ceases to grow when the seed is ripe. All parts of the seed lose water and by the time the seed is fully ripe all the physiological activities of the embryo and surrounding living cells are reduced to a minimal level. Once the ripened seeds are shed, a few are able to germinate immediately but the majoriy fail to germinate even when provided with the right conditions. The seed is said to be dormant. There are two descriptions of dormancy
— failure of a plant to germinate even when given suitable environmental conditons, due to inhibiting factors within the seed, and
— the ability of a seed to remain alive, though dry, for considerable periods of time, from only a few hours to hundreds of years.

A seed from the Indian Lotus germinated after 237 years of dormancy when it was accidentally soaked during a bombing raid on the British Museum in 1940. Even longer periods of dormancy have been recorded.

*SAQ 111* In what circumstances could it be of advantage to a plant for its seeds to lie dormant for a long time?

The most important conditions needed for the germination of a seed are a sufficient supply of water and oxygen and a suitable temperature. The exact requirements vary from plant to plant, but the first stage in germination is always the absorption of water.

The dry seed may have as little as ten per cent of water but once water becomes available, a large amount is quickly absorbed. For example, broad bean seeds absorb as much as one hundred and fifty per cent of their original weight.

A frequent cause of dormancy is the failure of water and oxygen to reach the living tissues of the seed. This is true for seeds of gorse, sweet pea and clover among others.

*SAQ 112* What structure(s) might cause seeds to be impermeable to the entrance of water and oxygen?

*SAQ 113* Suggest two ways in which this condition might be altered while the seed is lying in the soil.

Light has a variable effect on germination. Many seeds germinate equally well in light or darkness but others will only germinate successfully when exposed to light for some period. These seeds are said to be **light sensitive.** Those seeds that will only germinate in dark conditions are described as **light hard.** Seeds which require light in order to germinate are often relatively small.

*SAQ 114* Suggest an explanation for this fact.

When pasture land is ploughed up many weeds characteristic of arable land usually appear.

*SAQ 115* Suggest a reason for this occurrence.

Some seeds possess a dormancy which can usually only be terminated by exposure to a period of very low temperature (below 5 °C).

*SAQ 116* In what part of the world are such seeds likely to be produced and how might this requirement be an advantage for survival?

*SAQ 117* Suggest a dormancy factor which would be of advantage to the seeds of plants which grow in deserts. Explain your answer.

It has already been stated that water is essential for any germination to occur. Your observations in Practical Q will have shown you that uptake of water by the seed is considerable and rapid. Water is required to convert the living, but dry, protoplasm into an aqueous solution where enzymes can be functional and through which substances may diffuse.

*SAQ 118* From your observations, what other necessary event is brought about through water uptake?

Study the graph in figure 115

**115   Germinating barley: levels of amylase and starch per seed**

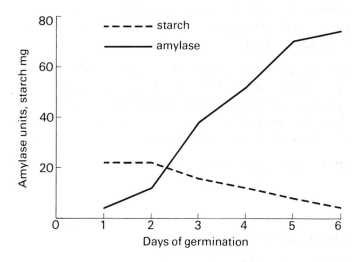

*SAQ 119* Explain the significance of the curves for amylase units per seed and for milligrams of starch per seed.

*SAQ 120* Why is starch suitable as a storage product in seeds?

*SAQ 121* Into what substances are starch, fats and proteins likely to be converted during early germination?

*SAQ 122* Relate the need for oxygen in germination to your answer to SAQ 119.

*SAQ 123* If the process of germination is measured by taking the dry mass of seeds, a clear decrease in mass is always observed over the period from the beginning of germination until the first green leaves are produced. Explain this result.

## 7.4 Summary assignment 10

1 Draw an annotated diagram of a named dicotyledonous seed to summarise the structure and function of its parts.
2 Write an essay plan to answer the question 'Describe the types of germination existing in dicotyledonous plants and the conditions needed for germination to occur'. Discuss this essay plan with your tutor before writing the essay.

Show this work to your tutor.

## 7.5 Primary growth in dicotyledonous plants

In section 1.7 you studied the early stages of primary growth of plant cells, namely growth by cell division, growth by cell expansion and, finally, the development brought about by the differentiation of cells. It is this last stage that will now be studied in more detail. Differentiation is largely associated with changes occurring in the cell walls which influence the living protoplasm of the cell. Your observations in practical B will have revealed some of the early changes in cell walls. The cell wall of typical living plant cells is thin and transparent and often less than 1 $\mu$m thick. It consists of the cell plate laid down first in cell division — a layer mainly of calcium pectate which becomes the **middle lamella** and, on either side of this, the cytoplasm deposits a meshwork of microfibrils composed of bundles of cellulose molecules cemented together with hemi-cellulose and other substances (see figure 116).

**Parenchyma** cells which form the chief tissue of fruits, flowers, pith and other unspecialised parts of stems and roots retain this simple primary cell wall within which lies the thin layer of living cytoplasm with its nucleus. The main bulk of the cell is occupied by the vacuole. The thin primary wall strongly resists stretching, however, and fully turgid parenchyma tissue plays an important role in mechanical support.

**Collenchyma** cells have extra layers of cellulose distributed unevenly in the wall and retain their living contents also. They serve a strengthening

*(a)* **Diagrammatic LS**

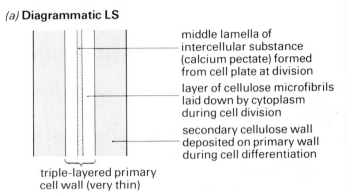

middle lamella of intercellular substance (calcium pectate) formed from cell plate at division

layer of cellulose microfibrils laid down by cytoplasm during cell division

secondary cellulose wall deposited on primary wall during cell differentiation

triple-layered primary cell wall (very thin)

*(b)* **Diagrammatic TS**

secondary wall

middle lamella

primary cellulose layer

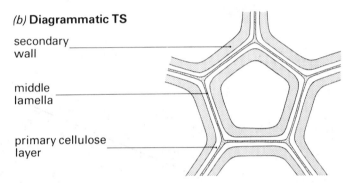

function and are usually found in the outer layers of stems and petioles. Figure 117 illustrates the appearance of these relatively undifferentiated living tissues.

The secondary wall is heavy and rigid with a compact regular arrangement of cellulose microfibrils. Secondary walls usually become impregnated with a complex organic compound called **lignin.** This is the substance which makes up the greater part of wood. Lignin is not immediately laid down throughout the whole of the cell wall so that distinct patterns of lignification can be recognised. When the secondary wall is formed, the living contents of the cell die. There are always certain areas of the cell wall where no lignin is deposited. These unthickened spots are known as **pits.** The process of differentiation will be studied in greater detail in section 7.5.2.

## 117　Relatively undifferentiated plant tissues

**Parenchyma cell**

thin primary cellulose wall

air-filled intercellular space

cell vacuole

cytoplasm

nucleus

**Collenchyma cell**

unevenly thickened cellulose wall

cell vacuole

cytoplasm

nucleus

## 118　TS of young root of *Vicia faba:* photomicrograph and plan

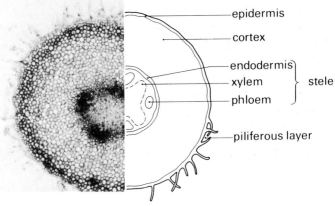

epidermis

cortex

endodermis
xylem
phloem
} stele

piliferous layer

*(a)* **Photomicrograph** (× **40**)　　*(b)* **Plan diagram**

## 119　TS of central portion of a root of *Ranunculus* sp.

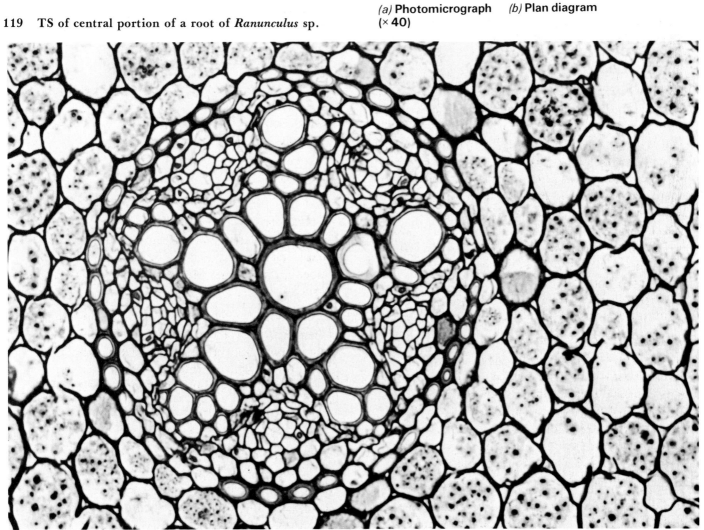

### 7.5.1 The cells and tissues formed in the primary growth of the root and stem

Figure 118(a) is a photomicrograph of a transverse section of a young *Vicia faba* root taken through the root-hair zone and showing an early stage of growth.

It is now possible to see that cells in different regions of the root have developed differently to form tissues which can be represented in a plan drawing (figure 118(b)).

The differentiation of these tissues represents primary growth. Figure 119, which shows the central portion of a *Ranunculus* root demonstrates these tissues.

A stem shows similarly differentiated tissue in the stage of primary growth though its pattern of distribution differs. The vascular tissue of a dicotyledonous stem is arranged in bundles towards the periphery of the stem. Figure 120 shows the arrangement of tissues in a young *Helianthus* stem. Figure 121 shows a portion of this stem at a higher magnification.

*SAQ 124* Compare the arrangement of primary vascular tissue in a root and a stem of a dicotyledonous plant.

### 7.5.2 Meristem of the stem apex

The source of cells for tissue differentiation is the meristem. The apical meristem at the growing tip of the stem consists of layers of small non-vacuolated cells. The outermost layers develop into either epidermal cells or young leaves. The young leaves grow initially to envelop and protect the apical region forming an apical bud. As the apical region extends, the leaves are left behind in position on the main stem and axillary buds form in the angle between the leaf and stem. These buds may give rise to side branches (see figure 122).

The cells that will form the vascular tissue begin to differentiate close behind the meristem but they do not originate from the central dome of the meristem. They form columns below the cells which give rise to leaves or branches, the leaf or branch **primordia.** From here, further columns of cells differentiate into

**120   TS young *Helianthus* stem**

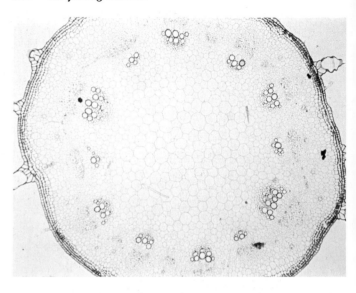

**121   TS portion of young *Helianthus* stem**

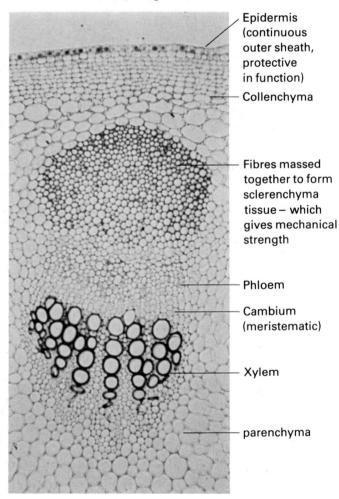

Epidermis (continuous outer sheath, protective in function)

Collenchyma

Fibres massed together to form sclerenchyma tissue – which gives mechanical strength

Phloem

Cambium (meristematic)

Xylem

parenchyma

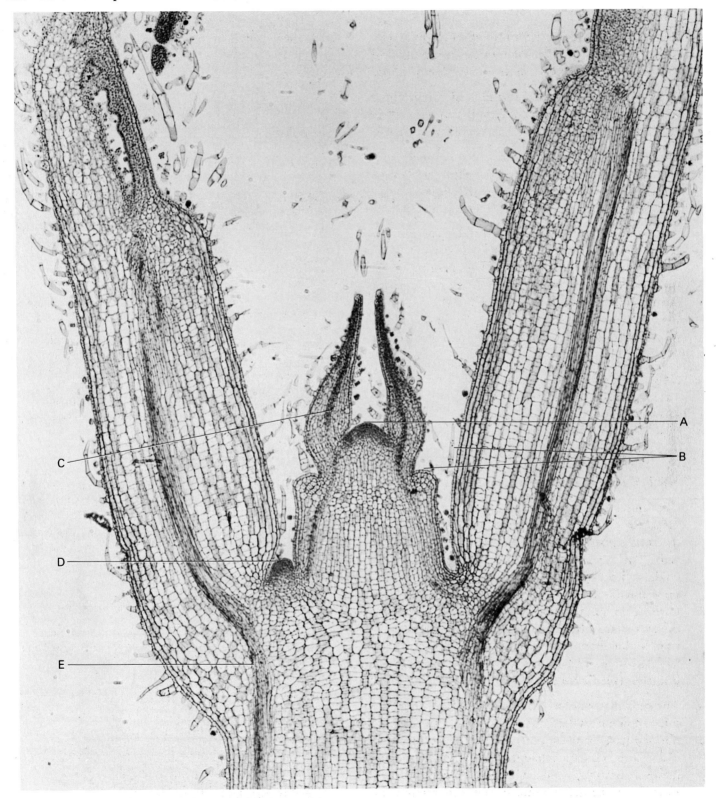

A

B

C

D

E

the developing leaves. These early stages of vascular development are called **procambial strands.**

*SAQ 125* Name the structures labelled **A, B, C, D** and **E** in the photomicrograph in figure 122.

### 7.5.3 The differentiation of phloem and xylem cells

Each mature cell in an organism, no matter how specialised it has become, retains its original genetic make-up. The chromosomes in a mature cell have been copied from the original set in the zygote. Despite this identical potential, cells mature to have very different structures and functions.

The phloem and xylem cells in the vascular bundles develop from the cells of the procambial strands.

Phloem develops from the outer side of the procambial strand, whilst xylem develops from the inner side.

This difference in position determines whether a cell will become, for example, a dead xylem vessel concerned with water and mineral transport or a living phloem tube concerned with nutrient transport. It is generally true for all plant and animal cells that the position of a cell and its interactions with neighbouring cells are decisive in its future development.

123   Summary diagram — differentiation of xylem and phloem

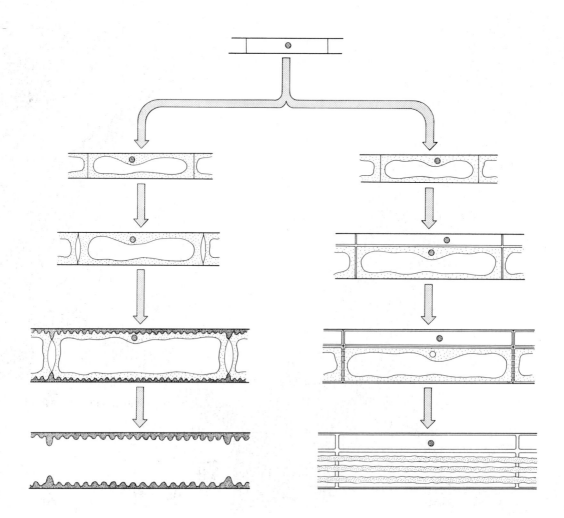

## 7.6 Summary assignment 11

Copy figure 123, showing the stages in differentiation of phloem and xylem cells. Refer to the diagram as you read through the rest of this sub-section and then label and annotate it to summarise the differentiation of these tissues.

Show this work to your tutor.

*Differentiation of phloem*

The first noticeable change in the procambial cell as it grows is the appearance of a vacuole. At this point, there is no apparent difference between phloem and xylem and at this early stage the cells are separated only by two thin primary walls joined by the middle lamella.

The phloem cells divide to cut off a small cell along one side called a companion cell. The primary cell walls continue growing and, as both cells increase in size, the nucleus of the sieve tube member (the larger cell) degenerates. The end walls of the cells now begin to break down at vaious points and the cytoplasm of adjacent cells appears to be connected by strands. The companion cells also appear to have cytoplasmic connections with the sieve tubes.

In the final stages of differentiation, obvious pores are formed in the connecting end walls which are now called sieve plates. The membrane around the vacuole breaks down. Figure 124 shows a fully differentiated sieve tube member with its companion cell.

**124    Sieve tube member and companion cell**

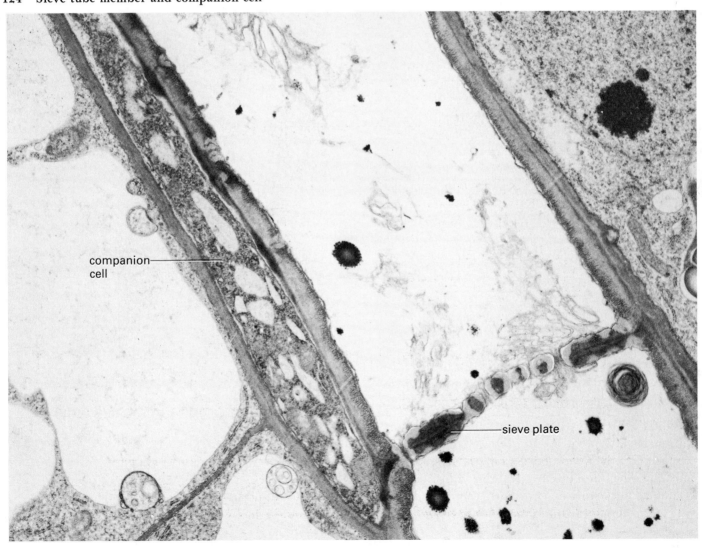

companion cell

sieve plate

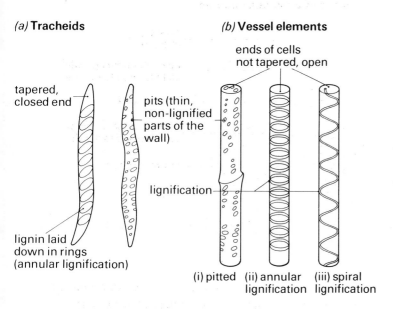

*(a)* **Tracheids**  *(b)* **Vessel elements**

tapered, closed end

pits (thin, non-lignified parts of the wall)

ends of cells not tapered, open

lignification

lignin laid down in rings (annular lignification)

(i) pitted  (ii) annular lignification  (iii) spiral lignification

*Differentiation of xylem*

Unlike phloem, xylem remains as one cell in its early stages of development. The first distinguishing change which occurs is the swelling of the middle lamella at its end walls. This area progressively enlarges and eventually the end walls break down completely forming the transverse perforation plate. The way in which adjacent xylem cells are joined at the transverse perforation plate defines whether the cell is a xylem vessel element or tracheid. These cells are illustrated in figure 125. Note that there is no direct connection between the end walls of tracheids.

Changes are also occurring along the side walls of the xylem cells during the later stages of differentiation. Secondary wall material (cellulose, hemi-cellulose and lignin) is deposited on the inner side of the primary cell wall. The lignin component, which is added last, cements the polysaccharides together and also renders the wall impermeable to water and solutes.

Lignified ribs are laid down on the inside of the walls which give the tubes added strength. These ribs can be laid down in a number of forms but spiral and annular thickening is particularly common (see figure 125). Sometimes lignification is more widespread but

during the process pits may be formed. These are areas of the cell where no secondary wall is present. Pits allow the passage of water and solutes. These are shown in figure 126.

The contents of the xylem cells break down, leaving a hollow tube.

126 **EM of pitted xylem vessel with perforation plate**

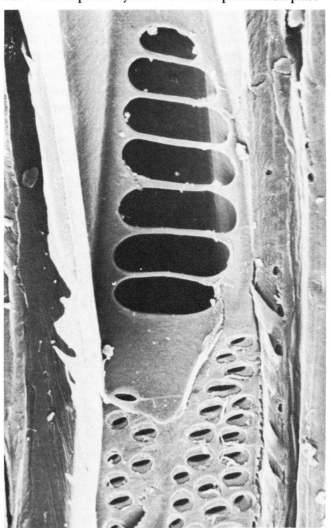

## 7.7 Secondary growth in dicotyledonous plants

Secondary growth is most common in dicotyledonous plants. It results in a thickening of the plant in contrast to primary growth which brings about an increase in length. Secondary growth originates in

**127** TS through part of a *Helianthus* stem at an early stage of secondary growth

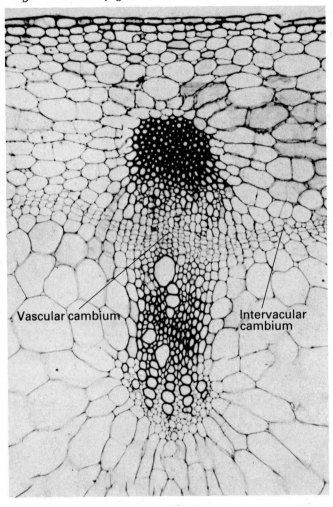

Vascular cambium     Intervacular cambium

**128** The formation of secondary vascular tissue in a segment of a vascular bundle

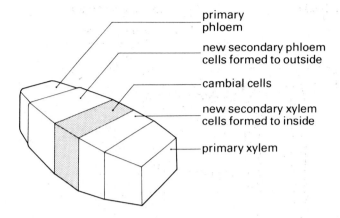

- primary phloem
- new secondary phloem cells formed to outside
- cambial cells
- new secondary xylem cells formed to inside
- primary xylem

lateral meristems which contain cambium cells developed from cells formed in primary growth.

Little is known about the mechanism which starts the secondary growth. The cells which become meristematic have obviously been formed as a result of primary growth which will still be going on at the tips of the plants. These cells begin a second wave of growth by starting to divide, thus forming a lateral meristem.

Secondary growth can be recognised from the time at which cells between the vascular bundles develop into cambial cells. This is known as intervascular cambium and it forms a complete cylinder with the vascular cambium within the original vascular

bundle. This cylinder is the lateral meristem and, as the cells divide, they form cylinders of secondary phloem cells to the outside and xylem cells to the inside (see figure 128).

The stages of division, expansion and differentiation which occur in primary growth also occur in secondary growth.

*SAQ 126* (*a*) List three differences between primary and secondary growth.

(*b*) What would you predict would be the effect of secondary growth on the primary phloem and xylem?

Figure 127 showed the early stages of secondary growth in the stem of a herbaceous dicolyledon, *Helianthus annuus* (sunflower). The resulting tissue formation from the early stages can be seen in figure 129.

As the secondary growth process continues, the delicate phloem cells are pushed outwards and become compressed, eventually collapsing. The xylem cells are strengthened with cellulose and lignin and eventually become the dominant tissue (see figure 130).

In Figure 130, two further features of secondary thickening can be seen, one of which is the parenchyma rays running from the cortex to the pith. These are plates of living cells.

**129   TS through part of a *Helianthus* stem showing secondary growth**

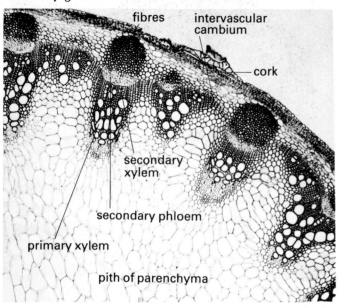

*Labels: fibres; intervascular cambium; cork; secondary xylem; secondary phloem; primary xylem; pith of parenchyma*

*SAQ 127* What function could be served by these parenchyma cells?

The second feature is the cork layer which has replaced the epidermis and cortex cells. This layer is formed in the woody as well as the herbaceous dicotyledons (see figure 130).

### 7.7.1 Formation of cork

After secondary thickening has begun in the stem, the epidermis and cortex are gradually replaced by cork. These cells are formed from a cork cambium just below the epidermis (see figure 131). Cork cells are dead and usually have no intercellular spaces. They have a protective function preventing water, gases and microorganisms passing through. They can do this because of the wax-like substance, suberin, which lines their walls. Pores called lenticels are present in the cork to make gas exchange possible. Their structure is shown in figure 131.

### 7.7.2 Woody dicotyledonous plants

Woody plants are different from herbaceous plants in their secondary growth. The cambium forms an almost complete ring of meristematic tissue during the primary growth phase. The parenchyma rays are

**130   TS through part of a *Helianthus* stem showing mature secondary growth**

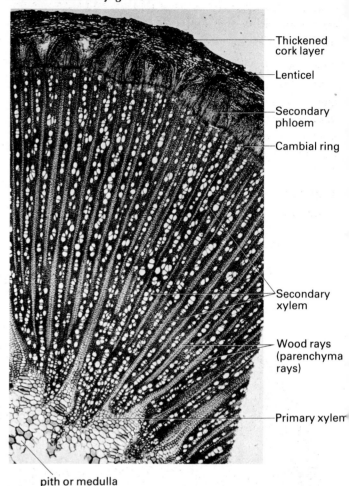

*Labels: Thickened cork layer; Lenticel; Secondary phloem; Cambial ring; Secondary xylem; Wood rays (parenchyma rays); Primary xylem; pith or medulla*

**131   TS lenticel**

*Labels: broken epidermis of the lenticel; loose suberised cells of the lenticel (allow passage of gases); bark; collenchyma of primary cortex; cork cambium (phellogen); cork*

very narrow and very little primary xylem or phloem is formed. Secondary growth soon begins and it is resumed each growing season (spring and summer in temperate climates). This type of growth is illustrated by figures 132 and 133.

The xylem formed first each growing season contains large, thin-walled vessels and fibres and is called early wood. Later in the season, smaller xylem vessels develop with thick walls to form late wood. It is this late wood which, having a dark, dense appearance, forms the annual growth ring (see figure 133).

*SAQ 128* How many years old is the twig shown in figure 133?

**132  TS of a stem of *Tilia vulgaris* (lime), one year old**

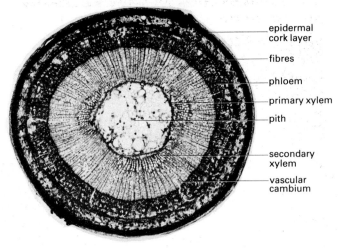

- epidermal cork layer
- fibres
- phloem
- primary xylem
- pith
- secondary xylem
- vascular cambium

**133  TS stem of *Tilia vulgaris***

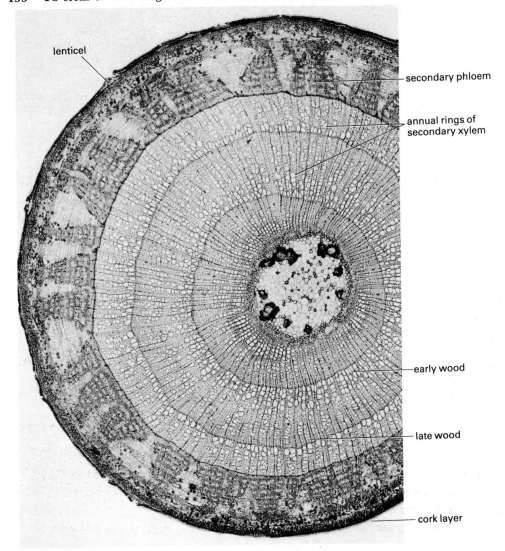

- lenticel
- secondary phloem
- annual rings of secondary xylem
- early wood
- late wood
- cork layer

### 7.7.3 Branching

Side (lateral) stems arise from lateral buds which are formed at the surface during primary growth. Their development is similar to that of the main stem with an apical meristem producing primary growth at the stem tip.

Lateral roots, however, arise from within the vascular tissue at the centre of the root. They are therefore referred to as endogenous ('inner formation') lateral roots, whilst the buds giving rise to lateral stems are called exogenous ('outer formation'). Figure 134 shows an endogenous lateral root developing.

*SAQ 129* Which tissues are involved in the formation of lateral roots?

---

**Practical R: Secondary growth in dicotyledonous stems**

---

### Materials

prepared slides (TS herbaceous dicotyledonous and woody dicotyledonous stems), microscope

### Procedure

(*a*) Set up your microscope and view each slide in turn.
(*b*) Choose one of the slides and draw a tissue plan of it.
(*c*) Annotate the tissue plan to illustrate clearly the changes occurring in secondary growth.
(*d*) Repeat stages (*b*) and (*c*) for the other slide.

Show this work to your tutor.

## 7.8 Further reading

*The Anatomy and Activities of Plants* by C.J. Clegg and Gene Cox.
*Photomicrographs of the Flowering Plant* by A.C. Shaw, S.K. Lazell and G.N Foster.

## 7.9 Summary assignment 12

Draw labelled tissue maps of (*a*) LS dicotyledonous stem apex showing primary growth, (*b*) TS dicotyledonous root showing primary growth, (*c*) TS dicotyledonous stem showing secondary growth. Add annotations to describe the nature of the cell walls in each region labelled and the similarities and differences in branching within each organ.

Show this work to your tutor.

Self test 8, page 111, covers section 7 of this unit.

**134   TS root of *Vicia* with developing lateral root**

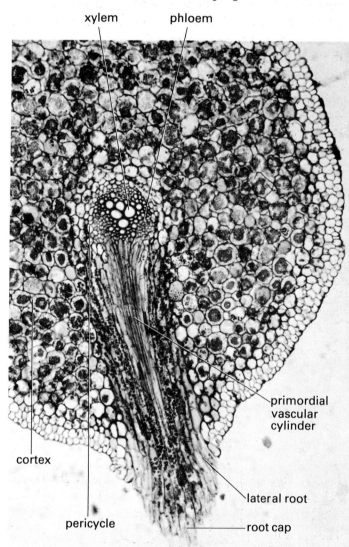

# Section 8 Plant life-cycles

## 8.1 Introduction and objectives

Most organisms undergo definite changes as they develop from fertilisation to maturity and finally die. In the course of its complete cycle an organism will grow, develop and usually reproduce. Cell division, both mitotic and meiotic will be involved in these processes. This section looks at the life-cycles of plants and studies the patterns that are shown in these cycles.

After working through this section, you should be able to do the following:

(*a*) Define the terms gametophyte, sporophyte and heterospory.
(*b*) Identify where meiosis and mitosis occur in the life-cycle of:
(i) a unicellular alga, e.g. *Pleurococcus;*
(ii) *Spirogyra;*
(iii) mosses and ferns;
(iv) conifers and angiosperms.
(*c*) Explain what is meant by alternations of generations.
(*d*) Compare the diploid phase of a moss, a fern and an angiosperm.

## 8.2 Life-cycles and cell division

A cell which divides mitotically will produce two identical cells. A dividing cell with $n$ chromosomes will give rise to two daughter cells each with $n$ identical chromosomes. Consider where mitosis occurs in the life of a unicellular alga such as *Pleurococcus* (see figure 135).

In *Pleurocuccus,* reproduction occurs by means of mitotic cell division. Each parent cell divides mitotically to produce two identical daughter cells.

In contrast, when a cell in an organism divides meiotically, four daughter cells are produced, each having half the chromosome number of the parent

**136   Life-cycle of *Spirogyra* showing where cell division occurs**

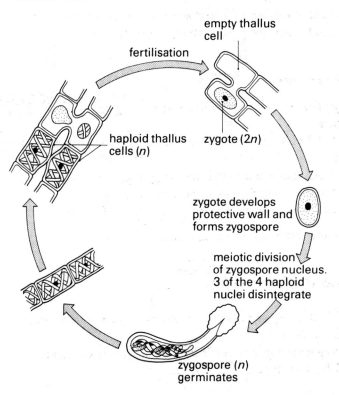

**135   Cell division in *Pleurococcus***

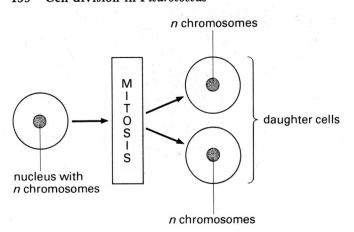

cell, and also different combinations of the maternal and paternal chromosomes inherited from previous generations due to independent assortment and crossing-over. Cells with half the parental chromosome number are called haploid cells. Consider where meiosis occurs in the life-cycle of *Spirogyra* (see figure 136).

**SAQ 130** Study figure 136 and answer the following questions:
Name the type of cell division which occurs
(a) at the first division of the zygospore;
(b) in the production of a multicellular filament from the zygospore.

The life-cycle of *Spirogyra* differs in several respects from that of mosses, ferns and angiosperms but it does illustrate important principles about the chromosome numbers in gametes and zygotes.

**SAQ 131** State what these principles are.

**SAQ 132** The life-cycle of mosses and ferns show a pattern which is typical of that found in all higher plants. This is summarised in figure 137. Copy it into your notebook. Complete (i) to (v) by writing in *n* for haploid or *2n* for diploid.

**SAQ 133** This type of life-cycle differs from that found in lower plants (e.g. *Spirogyra*) in two main ways. State what these are.

**138 Comparison of diploid phases in *Spirogyra*, a moss and a fern**

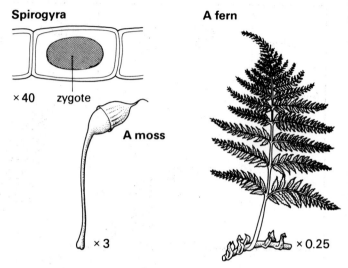

**SAQ 134** Figure 138 shows the diploid phase in *Spirogyra*, a moss and a fern. Compare and contrast each in terms of structural complexity and photosynthetic ability.

**SAQ 135** You have already studied the diploid phase of a moss and a fern in section 6. what special name was given to describe this phase and what does it tell about the function of the phase?

**SAQ 136** What name is given to the haploid phase of a moss or a fern?

## 8.3 Alternation of generations

These phases in the life of a plant are referred to as 'generations'.

A characteristic plant life-cycle can be drawn as shown in figure 139.

**139 Plant life-cycle**

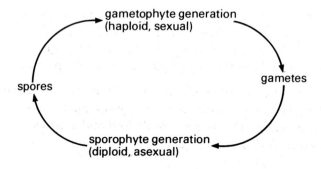

**137 The life-cycle of mosses, ferns and higher plants**

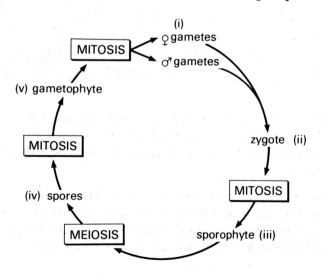

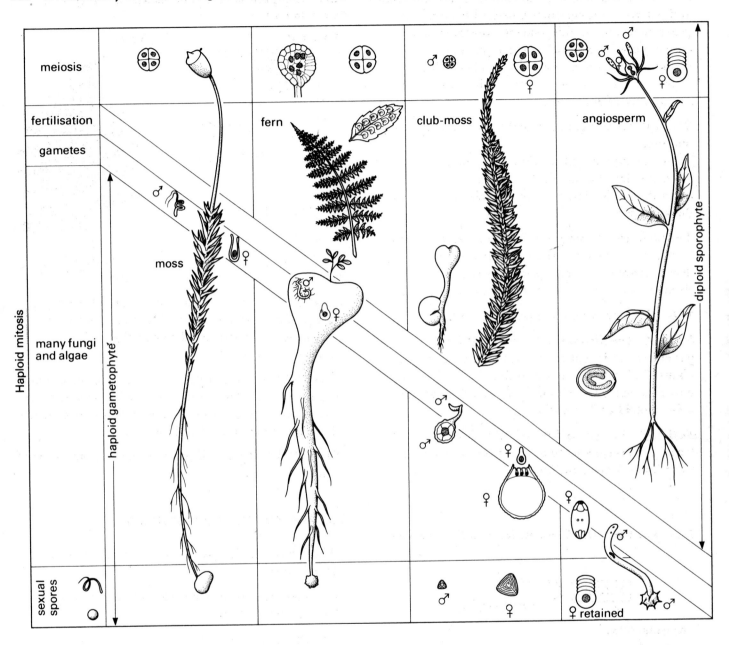

The generations alternate with one another giving rise to the term 'alternation of generations.' This type of life-cycle is found throughout the plant kingdom from the bryophytes to the angiosperms.

Alternation of generations is not found in the animal kingdom, even where asexual reproduction occurs. The animals themselves are diploid and meiosis occurs during gametogenesis.

In the lower plant groups, the gametophyte is the dominant generation and the sporophyte relatively insignificant. This means that the main plant body is haploid.

If a mutation occurs in a haploid organism it will have an immediate effect on the organism. Since most mutations are disadvantageous this may have a deleterious or even lethal effect. The effects of a mutation in a diploid organism may be masked by genes on the homologous chromosome. The diploid state also has advantages for the evolution of a population because the double chromosome number permits greater variation. The trend throughout the plant groups is for the sporophyte to become dominant. Thus, the 'fern' is a diploid sporophyte and the gametophyte is the small prothallus.

From pteridophytes onwards, the sporophyte is the dominant generation. This change in pattern can be related to the change from aquatic to terrestrial life. The evolution of the sporophyte generation is associated with the development of a waterproof cuticle. The differentiation of phloem and xylem cells for support and transport makes possible an increase in size. Land habitats are very varied and rapid changes in conditions may occur. The survivial of species in terrestrial environments requires adaptability and the range of variation of a diploid population makes this more likely.

Figure 140 illustrates the trend towards the dominance of the sporophyte generation and the reduction of the gametophyte in the plant groups.

You are already familiar with the life-cycles of mosses and ferns. Make sure that you can identify all structures represented in the columns for these groups. The club-mosses are also pteridophytes. Though today they are represented by small, leafy, evergreen plants, during the Carboniferous period, various tree-like forms flourished. Club-mosses possess a much reduced gametophyte generation but some species, for example, *Selaginella* are of interest because the gametophyte consists of separate male and female plants.

*Selaginella* produces two types of spore, large megaspores and the more numerous smaller microspores. The megaspore germinates to produce a female gametophyte which carries several archegonia but the microspores give rise to a male gametophyte which is reduced to only a few cells and bears a single antheridium.

Both types of gametophyte are microscopic and non-green. They are retained within the spore in which they form. The pattern of fertilisation is similar to that of ferns.

The production of unlike spores is referred to as **heterospory.**

Seed-bearing plants, the gymnosperms and angiosperms also show heterospory.

Using the above information together with figure 140, answer the following questions.

*SAQ 137* In what structures does meiosis occur (*a*) in a fern, (*b*) in an angiosperm?

*SAQ 138* Where does fertilisation occur in (*a*) a moss, (*b*) a club-moss?

*SAQ 139* What structure in a flowering plant is equivalent to (*a*) the megasporangium; (*b*) the microsporangium?

As figure 140 suggests, the gametophyte of flowering plants is greatly reduced and again is wholly retained within the sporophyte plant.

The female gametophyte is the embryo sac with its eight haploid nuclei. Refer back to section 5.4.

The male gametophyte is surrounded by the microspore which forms a wall. This structure is a pollen grain.

*SAQ 140* How do these developments better adapt angiosperms to life on land?

*SAQ 141* What is the main agent of dispersal in (*a*) bryophytes; (*b*) pteridophytes; (*c*) angiosperms?

*SAQ 142* After fertilisation, the ovule becomes a seed. List the advantages of seeds over spores in terms of (*a*) food reserves; (*b*) protection; (*c*) dispersal.

*SAQ 143* Explain how the life-cycle of angiosperms differs from that of mammals.

## 8.4 Summary assignment 13

The completed and corrected version of Self test 9 will provide a good summary for this section. File the Self test with your other summary assignments.

Self test 9, page 112, covers section 8 of this unit.

# Section 9 Growth and development in animals

## 9.1 Introduction and objectives

This section will give an outline of the processes of growth and development that are common to most multicellular animals. These processes are described in general terms but it should be borne in mind that multicellular animals are very diverse and that there are likely to be exceptions to most of these generalisations. Some animals display a special kind of development called metamorphosis and this is studied in insects and amphibians. Special attention is given to the role of hormones in the control of metamorphosis.

After working through this section you should be able to do the following;
(a) Describe the processes which occur in the growth and development of multicellular animals.
(b) Define the term metamorphosis.
(c) Explain the significance of metamorphosis in insects and amphibians.
(d) Outline the process of metamorphosis in
(i) a hemimetabolous (exopterygote) insect;
(ii) a holometabolous (endopterygote) insect;
(iii) a frog or toad.
(e) Give an account of the role of hormones in the control of metamorphosis of amphibians and insects.
(f) Predict the effect of certain experimental procedures on moulting and metamorphosis of insects.

### 141 Architecture of amphibian egg

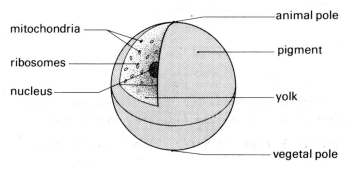

## 9.2 Embryonic growth and development

The event which normally initiates development in multicellular animals is the fertilisation of an egg by a sperm. Although in most vertebrates development of the egg is 'suspended' at metaphase of the second meiotic division it already has an ordered structure (see figure 141).

To some extent, the unfertilised egg possesses the necessary organisation to develop by itself and in some invertebrate groups, notably insects, development can proceed without sperm or fertilisation. The development of a new individual from an unfertilised egg is called **parthenogenesis.**

### 142 Cleavage in amphibian egg

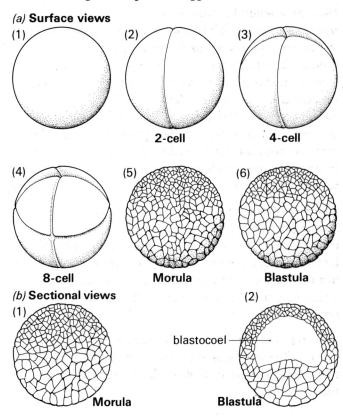

(a) **Surface views**
(1) (2) (3)
2-cell  4-cell
(4) (5) (6)
8-cell  Morula  Blastula
(b) **Sectional views**
(1) (2)
blastocoel
Morula  Blastula

Usually, however, further development is stimulated by the entry of a sperm at fertilisation. The entry of the sperm head activates the egg to repel other sperm, complete the second meiotic division and increase metabolism. Shortly after the joining of the two nucleii, the single-celled zygote enters the first stage of development termed **cleavage.** During this stage, the zygote divides by mitosis into a spherical mass of cells called the **morula.** See figure 142.

Eggs are extremely large when compared to other kinds of cell (the volume of the frog zygote is 1.6 million times larger than that of a normal frog cell) yet each contains only one nucleus. Thousands of cells and nucleii are formed by mitosis during cleavage but no growth occurs during this stage.

*SAQ 144* What is the important function of cleavage in the development of the organism?

As cleavage continues, a fluid-filled cavity called the **blastocoel** forms in the middle of the cell mass. Once the blastocoel has formed, the cell mass is called a **blastula** and the cleavage stage is regarded as being complete. See figure 142.

In the second stage of embryonic development, cell division continues but there is a coordinated movement of cells forming definite layers and masses. This stage is called **gastrulation** and the resulting 'cup-like' structure is termed a **gastrula.** See figure 143.

### 143   Gastrulation in amphibia

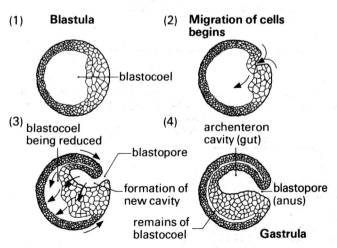

(1)   **Blastula**

(2)   **Migration of cells begins**

(3)   blastocoel being reduced — blastocoel, blastopore, formation of new cavity, remains of blastocoel

(4)   archenteron cavity (gut), blastopore (anus), **Gastrula**

### 144   Cell destination zones of the egg

**Sectional views of developing egg**

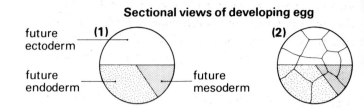

future ectoderm (1)

future endoderm

future mesoderm

(2)

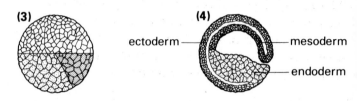

(3)

(4)   ectoderm — mesoderm — endoderm

Relatively little is understood about the control of cell migration during gastrulation. It seems that the position which any particular cell will end up at is actually determined during cleavage. See figure 144.

At the end of gastrulation in most of the invertebrates and all the vertebrates, the cell movements result in the formation of a three-layered (**triploblastic**) gastrula. The outer cell layer is the **ectoderm,** the inner layer the **endoderm** and the middle layer the **mesoderm.** See figure 145.

### 145   A triploblastic gastrula

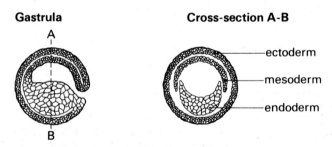

**Gastrula**

A

B

**Cross-section A-B**

ectoderm

mesoderm

endoderm

The third stage of early development involves the formation of organs. This results largely from the differentiation of cells of the mesoderm. The ectoderm gives rise to the skin and nervous system, whilst the endoderm is destined to become the lining of the internal organs.

The nuclei in all these cells are formed by mitosis and are therefore genetically identical and will have the same potential for development. How is it then that these cells can produce all the different organs of the adult organism? Look again at figures 141 and 142.

*SAQ 145* Explain how cells of the gastrula could, in fact, already be quite different from each other.

The smooth layers of cells formed in gastrulation seem to break up into separate masses, each of which will form an organ. One theory is that the cells of each mass attract each other, forming a particular shape, while repelling cells from different masses.

Figure 146 shows the pattern of progressive differentiation of cells from an unfertilised egg to mature tissues and organs in a vertebrate.

*SAQ 146* Which organ arises partly from
(*a*) mesoderm and endoderm;
(*b*) mesoderm and ectoderm?

The formation of all the various organs listed in figure 146 involves radical changes in structure and function of the cells involved. These changes may have been influenced by the differences between the cytoplasm of individual cells as has already been mentioned. However, the structure and function remain under the control of the genetic material within each cell.

**146   Progressive differentiation of cells during early development**

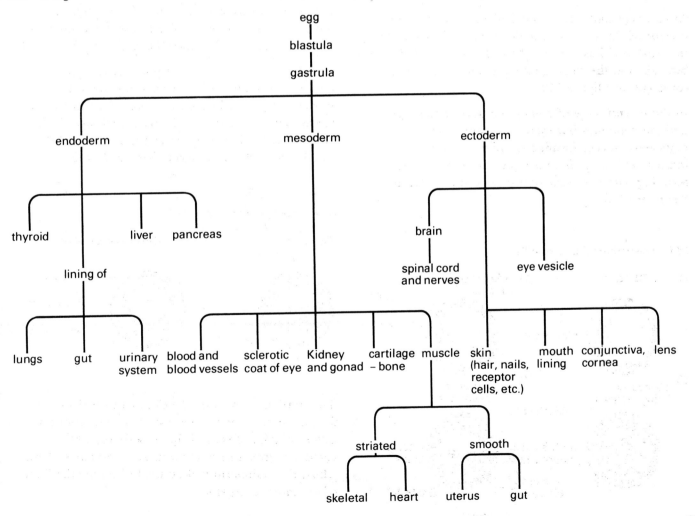

## 9.3 Summary assignment 14

After reading through the description of embryonic growth and development, construct a table which lists the stages in development, the major activity of each stage and the tissues or structures formed.

Show this work to your tutor.

## 9.4 Larvae and metamorphosis

Embryonic development usually ends in the hatching (more rarely birth) of the animal generally as a larval form. A **larva** is a stage in the development of the organism which, for a time, leads an active life usually quite unlike that lived by the adult. As you will see later, this has important implications for survival. Larvae represent a break in the steady continuity of development into the adult because the larva undergoes a post-embryonic reorganisation of tissues. This relatively brief period of development from larva to adult is called **metamorphosis.**

**147   Development from tadpole to frog**

| Approx. time after hatching | Development | Food | Gas exchange | Excretory product |
|---|---|---|---|---|
| 0 days (approx. 2 weeks after fertilisation) | 2 pairs external gills. No mouth. Sucker for attachment to weed | Yolk in endoderm cells | Diffusion through skin and gills. Haemoglobin with high $O_2$ affinity | Ammonia and some urea |
| 2–3 days | 3 pairs external gills. Mouth with horny lips adapted for scraping. Tail lengthens. Long coiled gut | Algae, pond-weed | | |
| 1 week onwards | 4 gill clefts open. Operculum begins to grow. Internal gills begin to grow. External gills wither. Sucker degenerates | | Respiratory current of water enters mouth, travels down pharynx, over gills in area covered by operculum. Out through spiracle. Also diffusion through skin | |
| 2 weeks | Period of growth. Limb buds appear at base of tail | | | |
| 4 weeks | Jointed hind-limbs present. Fore-limbs penetrate spiracle on left side and break through operculum on right side. Gut shortens | Gradual change to carnivorous diet | | |
| 8 weeks | Lungs developing. Gradual degeneration of gills | | | |
| 10 weeks | Outer layer of skin and horny jaws cast off. Mouth enlarges and changes shape, tongue grows longer | Carnivorous diet — pond animals | Visits surface for air-breathing. Haemoglobin shows less affinity for $O_2$ but unloads $O_2$ more readily. $O_2$ through skin, pharynx and lungs | |
| 3 months | Skin becomes keratinised, tail resorbed, head flattens, eyes enlarge and bulge. Leaves water | Worms, flies, etc | | Urea and some ammonia |

Metamorphosis prepares the larva for life in the habitat of the adult.

Three characteristics define a larva:
(*a*) it is different from the adult in structure and physiology;
(*b*) it is capable of leading an independent life in a habitat often very different from that of the adult;
(*c*) it is sexually immature.

*SAQ 147* What is the significance of these characteristics for the survival of the larva and adult?

**148  Change in appearance of a tadpole as it develops into a frog**

Larvae are generally one of two basic types:
(*a*) highly motile but with poorly developed mouthparts and digestive systems, e.g. barnacle larvae;
(*b*) highly efficient feeders with poorly developed locomotory stuctures, e.g. butterfly larvae.

*SAQ 148* What is the main function of each type of larva?

In land animals that have to return to water to reproduce, the larvae must have a form suited to its aquatic habitat. Metamorphosis allows the organism to move from the aquatic habitat essential for

**Right side views**

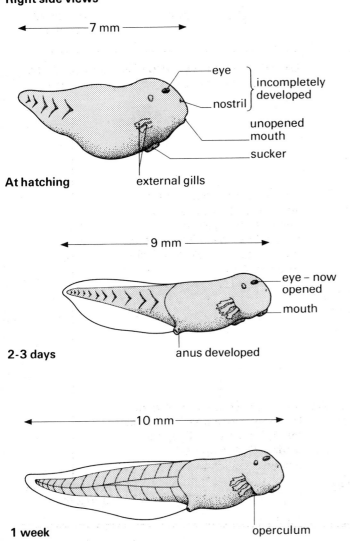

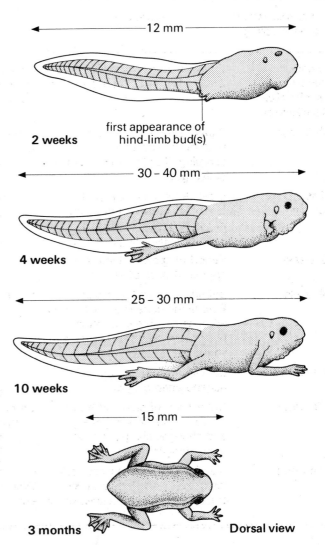

reproduction and early development to that of dry land.

One larval animal with which you are likely to be familiar is the tadpole. Figures 147 and 148 look at the development of a frog from egg to adult.

*SAQ 149* Explain how a tadpole fulfils the criteria for being called a larva.

*SAQ 150* Why should the young tadpole require a long gut while the tadpole about to metamorphose has a much shorter gut?

*SAQ 151* What biochemical developments may accompany this change?

*SAQ 152* Why does a tadpole's haemoglobin show a higher affinity for oxygen than that of a frog?

*SAQ 153* Why is ammonia a satisfactory excretory product for an aquatic animal but unsuitable for a terrestrial animal?

## 9.5 Amphibian metamorphosis and the thyroid gland

The thyroid gland is an endocrine gland that produces two similar hormones, **thyroxin** and **tri-iodothyronine**. Both these chemicals incorporate iodine in their molecules. A number of investigations have been performed on metamorphosis in the bullfrog, *Rana catesbeiana*.

### Investigation A

Newly-hatched tadpoles were injected with the hormone tri-iodothyronine. Figure 149 shows the observations made over a period of nine days.

In normal circumstances, tadpoles of the size used in the investigation take up to two years to complete metamorphosis.

*SAQ 154* Name two internal changes that are likely to have also taken place in the nine-day period.

*SAQ 155* For what purpose does the mouth size increase?

*SAQ 156* What part of the body accounts for the greatest decrease in length?

**149   Development of bullfrog tadpoles injected with tri-iodothyronine**

| Days after injection | Body length | Fore-limbs | Hind-limbs | Mouth size |
|---|---|---|---|---|
| 0 | 8.6 cm | absent | absent | 3 mm |
| 4 | 7.2 cm | 'bulges' visible | present | 5 mm |
| 9 | 5.3 cm | left fore-limb emerged | present | 12 mm |

### Investigation B

Sections were made of the thyroid gland of two tadpoles. Tadpole 1 had not yet reached the hind-limb stage of development, but buds were present.

Tadpole 2 already possessed hind-limbs and one fore-limb had emerged from its position under the **operculum** (the cover that grows over the gill slits).

The sections were stained and examined under a microscope. Figure 150 shows the observations and comparisons for tadpoles 1 and 2.

**150   Comparison of thyroid glands of two tadpoles at different stages of development**

| | Relative size of gland | Size of follicles | Appearance of follicle epithelium cells |
|---|---|---|---|
| Tadpole 1 | small | small with little lumen | flat or cubical cells |
| Tadpole 2 | size increase over 1 approx. × 5 | much larger with wide lumen | most cells columnar in shape |

Similar sections were obtained from other tadpoles and the same differences were observed. It is known that the shape of the follicle cells alters depending on their activity, columnar cells being most active in secreting thyroid hormones.

*SAQ 157* It is known that in amphibians, metamorphosis and the development of the thyroid gland are connected. On the basis of the evidence presented in investigations A and B, formulate an hypothesis about the thyroid gland and metamorphosis.

## Investigation C

Investigations have shown that if the thyroid gland is surgically removed from tadpoles, before or in the early stage of metamorphosis, they either do not begin to metamorphose, or metamorphosis is arrested at the stage when the removal occurred. When thyroid hormones are subsequently added to the water in which these tadpoles are living, metamorphosis begins or recommences.

**SAQ 158** Does this evidence support the hypothesis put forward in answer to question 157? Explain fully

Gudersnatch investigated metamorphosis in 1912. He removed various glands from vertebrates, made extracts and fed these to tadpoles before metamorphosis. An extract of sheep's thyroid greatly increased the rate of metamorphosis in the tadpoles.

**SAQ 159** What further information does this supply about the nature of vertebrate hormones?

Metamorphosis is seen as consisting of two phases. In the Common British Frog, *Rana temporaria*, metamorphosis takes about twelve weeks. The roughly nine-week phase from hatching until the hind legs are of equal length to the 'trunk' of the frog is referred to as **prometamorphosis.** The second stage includes emergence of the fore-limbs, the reabsorption of the tail and accompanying internal and biochemical changes. It is referred to as **metamorphic climax.** If thyrectomised tadpoles (those in which the thyroid gland has been removed) are placed in water containing a low dose of thyroxin, normal prometamorphosis occurs, but after that metamorphosis proceeds very slowly and sometimes fails to be completed. If the dose is increased by a factor of about twenty towards the end of prometamorphosis, metamorphic climax proceeds normally.

**SAQ 160** On this evidence, make a statement about the amounts of thyroid hormone required during metamorphosis.

**SAQ 161** What other piece of evidence already presented supports your statement?

In another line of investigation into the control of frog metamorphosis, the pituitary gland which is located in the brain, was removed from tadpoles. No metamorphosis occurred.

More recent research has revealed that the pituitary gland and a region of brain close to it, the **hypothalamus,** play an essential part in the regulation of hormone production by vertebrate endocrine glands. The hypothalamus produces **thyroid releasing factor** (TRF) which stimulates the pituitary to produce a hormone called **thyroid stimulating hormone** (TSH). When a barrier was placed between the brain and the pituitary gland, metamorphosis proceeded normally through its early stages (prometamorphosis) but was arrested just before metamorphic climax.

**SAQ 162** From the information above, suggest an explanation of the functioning of the pituitary and brain in regulating prometamorphosis and metamorphic climax.

**SAQ 163** Draw a diagram which shows the control of frog metamorphosis. The first part is done for you (see figure 151).

**151   Diagram for SAQ 163**

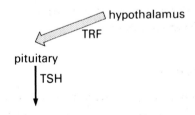

**Recommended reading**

Scientific American Offprint No. 170 – *The Chemistry of Amphibian Metamorphosis* by Earl Frieden.

## 9.6 Summary assignment 15

1 Using figures 147 and 148 make a record of frog metamorphosis in the form of annotated diagrams.
2 Make a record of the answer to SAQ 163.

Show this work to your tutor.

## 152 A moth: eggs, larva, pupa and adult showing main external features

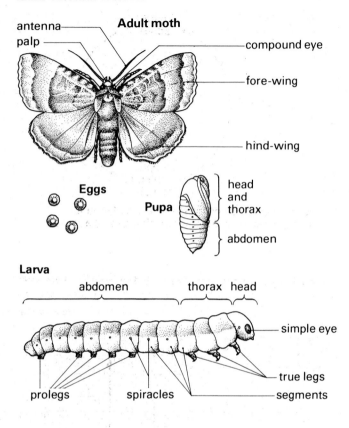

**Adult moth**

antenna
palp
compound eye
fore-wing
hind-wing

**Eggs**

**Pupa**

head
and
thorax

abdomen

**Larva**

abdomen | thorax | head

simple eye

true legs
segments

prolegs | spiracles

## 9.7 Growth and metamorphosis in insects

The growth of insects is accompanied by a series of moults or **ecdyses.** The soft parts of an insect are enclosed within an external skeleton or **cuticle** made primarily of chitin (a polysaccharide) hardened with **sclerotin** (a fibrous protein). A new chitinous cuticle, folded and compressed, forms beneath the old one, separated from it by a layer of liquid. This liquid absorbs the chitin from the old skeleton leaving the harder protein parts. The liquid and chitin are absorbed through the permeable new skeleton into the body of the insect. The old exoskeleton splits and is shed and the insect expands rapidly by swallowing air or water as long as the new cuticle is soft and elastic. Once this has hardened, the size remains fixed until the next moult. Some larval insects possess soft cuticles and in these cases increase in size may continue between moults.

Among the winged insects, the **Pterygota,** two distinct types of life-cycle exist. There are the insects that hatch from an egg in a form quite different in appearance from the adult, or **imago.** This immature form is called a larva and exhibits the characteristics mentioned in section 9.4. Figure 152 illustrates the difference in appearance between larva and imago in a moth.

After several moults the larva enters into a resting stage or **pupa** which is physically inactive, but during which radical reorganisation of the tissues takes place. This radical change is termed **complete metamorphosis** and the insects are said to be **holometabolous.** Alternatively, they are known as the **Endopterygota** because their wings develop internally. Examples include flies, moths, butterflies, bees, wasps and beetles.

Figure 153 shows the life-cycle of a holometabolous insect.

In the second type of life-cycle, insects such as the cockroach, grasshopper, dragonfly, mayfly and locust hatch from the egg in a form very much like that of the adult except for the absence of wings which develop externally at each successive moult. The young are referred to as **nymphs** or **instars** and lack mature sexual organs while possessing other adult features such as compound eyes (see figure 154). Thus, metamorphosis, though discernible, is com-

## 153 Life-cycle showing complete metamorphosis

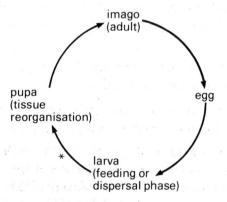

imago
(adult)

egg

pupa
(tissue
reorganisation)

*

larva
(feeding or
dispersal phase)

*growth of the larva may be accompanied by
a series of larval moults (shedding of exoskeleton)

**154 A locust: egg, nymphs and adult showing main external features**

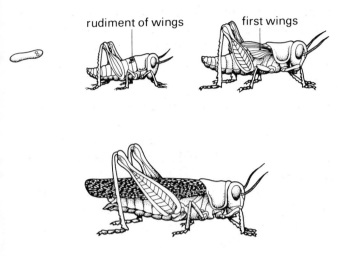

rudiment of wings

first wings

**155 Life-cycle showing incomplete metamorphosis**

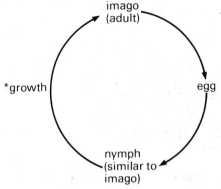

imago (adult)

egg

*growth

nymph (similar to imago)

*Growth is accompanied by a series of moults. At each moult developmental changes take place.

paratively slight and is termed **incomplete meta-morphosis.**

These insects are said to be **hemimetabolous.** They are also known as the **Exopterygota** because their wings develop externally.

Figure 155 shows the life-cycle of hemimetabolous insects.

The graph (figure 156) shows the changes of mass during development of an aquatic insect *Notonecta glauca* (waterboatman) with measurements taken every day.

*SAQ 164* How many instars does the insect develop through?

*SAQ 165* What is happening to account for the rapid increase in mass shown at, for example, days 36 and 52?

*SAQ 166* Why should this initial rapid increase in mass not be termed growth?

*SAQ 167* What must happen after such an increase in mass for true growth to occur?

Moulting of epidermal structures is also quite common in other animal groups. Amphibians and reptiles periodically shed outer layers of skin while birds and mammals often alter plumage or pelage according to season or reproductive state.

**156 Changes in mass during development of *Notonecta glauca***

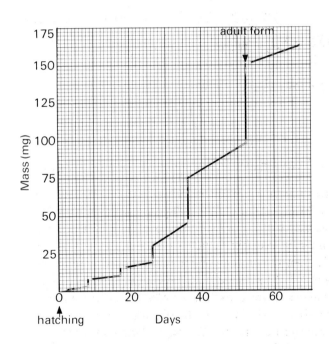

adult form

hatching    Days

## 9.8 Control of growth and metamorphosis in insects

Hormones play a very important role in the growth, moulting, pupation and metamorphosis of insects. There are a vast number of insect species and only a very small fraction of these have been investigated.

Nevertheless, there is a striking similarity in the functions of hormones in different insects. Hemimetabolous insects and holometabolous insects use exactly the same hormones.

In 1922, Kopec demonstrated that insect development was probably under hormonal control by tying tight ligatures at various positions along the body of the last larval stage of a moth. He discovered that when the ligature was tied before a certain critical period, the larva would pupate *anterior* to the ligature, but remained larval behind it. In other larvae, the cutting of the nerve cord had no effect on subsequent pupation, and he came to the conclusion that a **'pupa-inducing substance'** was produced by a tissue in the head end of the caterpillar and circulated through the body to bring about pupation. He tested various tissues and discovered that the removal of the brain prevented pupation. Re-implantation of the brain allowed it to proceed again. (Insects are very tolerant of drastic surgery which makes them ideal for investigations such as those that are described here.)

Wigglesworth carried out a thorough series of investigations on a South American blood-sucking bug, *Rhodnius,* see figure 157.

### 157   Two stages in the development of *Rhodnius*

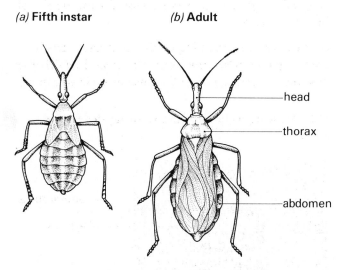

*(a)* **Fifth instar**          *(b)* **Adult**

head

thorax

abdomen

This insect hatches from the egg as a very small, blood-sucking nymph which goes through five instars, gradually developing into the adult form. A large meal of blood is required before moulting will occur.

### Investigation 1

Investigations involved decapitating nymphs at early intervals after a blood meal. Animals decapitated up to five days after the meal do not moult, but a gradually increasing number will moult if decapitation occurs *after* this critical time. If decapitation occurs after about the eighth day, all the nymphs will moult. See figure 158.

### 158   Treatment and results for investigation 1

| Time of decapitation after blood meal (days) | Percentage of nymphs that moult |
|:---:|:---:|
| 1 | 0 |
| 3 | 0 |
| 5 | 0 |
| 7 | 30 |
| 9 | 100 |
| 11 | 100 |

***SAQ 168*** How did the investigations in (1) develop the ideas on hormonal control of development a stage further than the investigations of Kopec? Explain your answer carefully.

### 159   Two *Rhodnius* nymphs decapitated and united

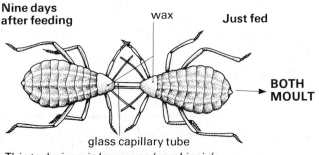

**Nine days after feeding**          wax          **Just fed**

**BOTH MOULT**

glass capillary tube

This technique is known as 'parabiosis'.
The insects so united have a common blood system

## Investigation 2

If a bug that has been decapitated nine days after feeding is united with another bug decapitated immediately after its blood meal, both insects will moult. See figure 159.

***SAQ 169*** How do the investigations in (2) support the idea developed by (1)?

## Investigation 3

Nine days after a blood meal, nymphs of *Rhodnius* were subjected to the following treatment. The head and thorax were removed from all the larvae, *then* Group A were left untreated. Group B had the thorax implanted into the abdomen. Group C had the head implanted into the abdomen. Group D had the head and thorax implanted into the abdomen. See figure 160.

***SAQ 170*** What new information and conclusions are provided by the results of investigation 3?

Further research has revealed the sequence of events involved in the moulting of *Rhodnius* nymphs.

A large blood meal distends the gut which stimulates a patch of **neurosecretory cells** (modified neurons that secrete hormones) in the insect brain. The hormone which can be called **'brain hormone'** does not directly trigger moulting but instead acts upon a pair of glands in the thorax, the **prothoracic glands.**

160    Treatment and results for investigation 3

| Treatment | | Result |
|---|---|---|
| head<br>thorax<br>developing wings<br>abdomen | A | no moult |
| | B | no moult |
| | C | no moult |
| | D | moult |

When stimulated by the 'brain hormone', the prothoracic glands produce a second hormone called **ecdysone** which directly initiates the changes in moulting.

Further investigations carried out by Wigglesworth led to an understanding of the control of metamorphosis that accompanies moulting in *Rhodnius*.

## Investigation 4

A fifth-stage nymph (stage before adult) that has had a blood meal is decapitated *after* the critical period and is connected to an intact first-stage nymph that has not yet fed. Both bugs will moult, the first instar becomes a normal second instar nymph but the fifth instar does not acquire adult features. See figure 161.

161    Treatment and results for investgation 4

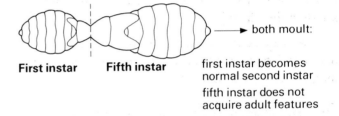

First instar    Fifth instar    both moult:

first instar becomes normal second instar

fifth instar does not acquire adult features

***SAQ 171*** Suggest a possible reason for the results of investigation 4.

As early as the beginning of this century, a small pair of glands *behind* the brain had been identified as possible endocrine glands because of their structure.

162    View of an insect brain showing the corpora allata

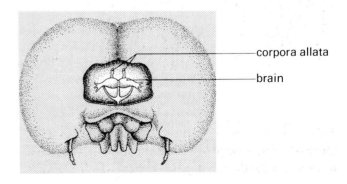

corpora allata

brain

See figure 162. These glands were called the corpora allata (singular: corpus allatum).

When the corpora allata are removed from early instar nymphs, moulting occurs as usual but instead of the next stage nymph, a small adult emerges.

**SAQ 172** If the corpora allata of a fourth instar *Rhodnius* were implanted into a fed fifth instar *Rhodnius,* what kind of stage would you expect to appear at the next moult?

**SAQ 173** What do you think is the normal function of the corpora allata?

As you have seen, moulting and metamorphosis are regulated in the same general way and are therefore usually studied together. But remember we are dealing with two separate processes, the shedding of cuticle and the expression of adult features.

Normally, an adult *Rhodnius* does not moult, but if large amounts of the 'brain hormone' which stimulates the production of ecdysone are injected into it, it will moult. If the hormone produced by the corpora allata is applied to the insect's exoskeleton, the part affected will revert to the juvenile form at the next moult.

In a similar investigation, Wigglesworth painted his initials on an adult *Rhodnius* with the corpora allata hormone which has been given the name **juvenile hormone.** After the forced moult, the initials could be read because of the contrast between the areas of juvenile and adult cuticle (see figure 163).

**SAQ 174** (*a*) Which hormone caused the insect to moult?
(*b*) Which hormone was responsible for the larval areas of the cuticle?

**SAQ 175** Note down the names of the hormones (1) to (3) in figure 164.

**SAQ 176** Think carefully about figure 164 and all the other evidence you have read in this section. Suggest how development in *Rhodnius* is controlled.

**Recommended reading**

Scientific American Offprint No. 63 – *Metamorphosis and Differentiation* by V.B. Wigglesworth.

**163 Local inhibition of metamorphosis in *Rhodnius***

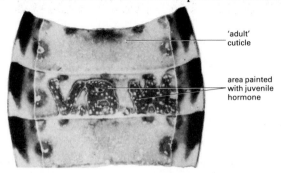

'adult' cuticle

area painted with juvenile hormone

**164 Control of moulting and metamorphosis in *Rhodnius***

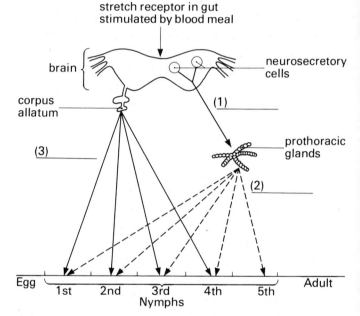

stretch receptor in gut stimulated by blood meal

brain

neurosecretory cells

corpus allatum

(1)

(3)

prothoracic glands

(2)

Egg    1st    2nd    3rd    4th    5th    Adult
Nymphs

## 9.9 Summary assignment 16

1 Copy and complete labelling in figure 164.
2 The following question comes from the University of London examination paper for June 1979. Answer the question concisely. You may use note form.
(*a*) What are the essential features of the complete metamorphosis in a *named* insect?
(*b*) Explain briefly how the life-cycle of an insect with incomplete metamorphosis differs from that of an insect with complete metamorphosis.
(*c*) Give an account of the ways in which insect metamorphosis is controlled..

Use clearly-labelled diagrams wherever this is useful.

Show this work to your tutor.

Self test 10, page 114, covers section 9 of this unit.

# Section 10 Self tests

## Self test 1

1 Read through the following account of mitosis and then supply the most appropriate word or words to complete the account.

Mitosis is the division of a (1) to give two (2) of identical (3) composition. During the first stage of this process, known as the (4) the chromosomes shorten and (5). They can also be seen to have divided lengthwise into (6). The next stage of the process is marked by the membrane of the (7) breaking down and the chromosomes moving towards the (8) of the spindle. The chromosomes become attached to (9) fibres. Meanwhile, the (10) divide, initiating the drawing apart of the 'daughter' chromosomes towards the opposite (11) of the spindle. Each group of new chromosomes becomes part of a new nucleus and the chromosomes now become less easily (12). In plant cells, a cell (13) separates the two new cells, whilst in animal cells the (14) cuts across between the nuclei.

2 Figure 165 represents a mitotic cell. Name the parts labelled **A  B  C,** and **D.**

3 Draw a diagram of a cell showing four chromosomes at the metaphase stage of nuclear division. Label your diagram to show the equator and poles of the spindle apparatus.

### 165   A mitotic cell

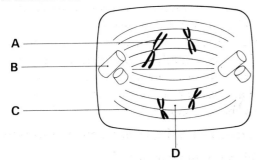

4 The photomicrographs (figure 166) are of the different stages of mitosis in a plant cell. Indicate the name of each stage and place them in their correct sequence.

### 166   Photomicrographs of stages in mitosis

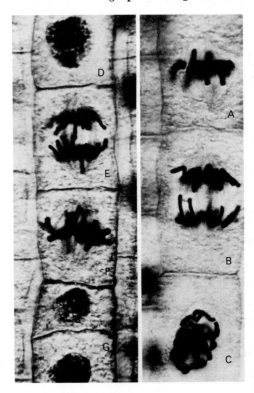

## Self test 2

1 Distinguish between growth of individuals and growth of a population.

2 Explain the difference between differentiation and development.

3 Is it possible to get an increase in size and a decrease of (a) wet mass, (b) dry mass? Give reasons for your answer.

4 Replication of genetic material during the mitotic cycle is thought to occur during:

interphase                  metaphase
prophase                   early anaphase?

**167 Diagram for question 6**

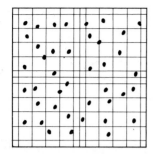

5 Where does most growth occur in a root?
(*a*) At the extreme tip of the root.
(*b*) At a region just behind the root tip.
(*c*) Evenly throughout the root.
(*d*) Near to the mid-region of the root.
6 Estimate the density of bacteria in the culture shown on a haemocytometer slide (figure 167).
7 Draw a sigmoid growth curve and label its three main phases.
8 List five external factors which influence growth.
9 Briefly compare the distribution of growing cells in mature flowering plants and mammals.
10 List the three phases of primary growth in plant cells.

## Self test 3

1 Give two differences and one similarity between asexual and sexual reproduction.
2 Name three environmental conditions in which asexual reproduction commonly occurs.
3 Supply one difference between binary fission in *Paramecium* and *Euglena*. Name two other organisms that reproduce by binary fission.
4 Match the following organisms to their method of asexual reproduction:
(i) hairmoss              **A** sporulation
(ii) sea anemone      **B** budding
(iii) spirogya            **C** fragmentation
(iv) toadstool
5 Explain the difference between the following pairs of terms:
(*a*) Runners and suckers.
(*b*) Bulbs and corms.
(*c*) Rhizomes and stem tubers.

6 What is the difference between perennation and asexual reproduction?
7 The main advantage of propagating roses by budding is that this
(*a*) encourages species to hybridise,
(*b*) reproduces the strain,
(*c*) gives rise to new varieties,
(*d*) increases the chance of somatic mutation at the graft site.
8 Name two factors essential for a successful graft.
9 Distinguish between rootstock and scion.
10 How is asexual reproduction closely linked with the growth process?

## Self test 4

1 List the four main events which must take place if sexual reproduction is to occur.
2 Copy, and complete the blanks in figure 168 so that it provides a summary of meiosis.

**168 Diagram for question 2**

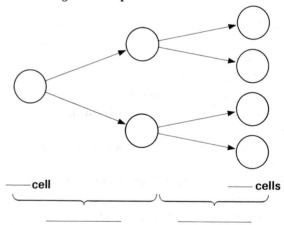

——cell                                    ——cells

3 In which of the following tissues does meiosis *not* occur?
Ovary, testes, anther, stigma.
4 Figure 169 represents oogenesis. Copy it and complete all the blanks. Add a line to show when meiosis occurs.
5 In flowering plants, which cell undergoes meiosis to produce (*a*) female gametes, (*b*) male gametes?

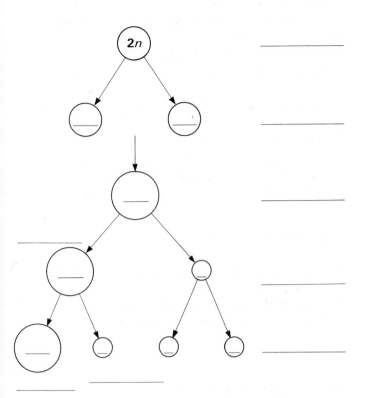

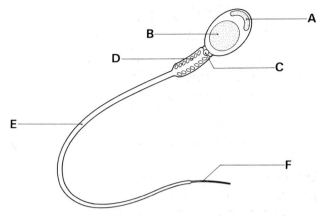

10 Why may sexual reproduction provide a means of survival for a species in unfavourable or changing conditions?

6 The diagram (figure 170) shows a spermatazoon. Write down the letter which indicates each of the following:
(i) the genetic information;
(ii) the part concerned with energy release;
(iii) the portion which resembles a cilium in structure;
(iv) the portion concerned with penetration of the egg.
7 Are eggs and sperm heterogametes or isogametes? Explain your answer.
8 Explain the difference between internal and external fertilisation. Give three advantages of internal fertilisation over external fertilisation.
9 List the words to complete the gaps in the following statements.
(a) An animal which produces both male and female gametes is said to be _____.
(b) A plant which has both stamens and ovules is said to be _____.
(c) The development of an ovum, without fertilisation to produce a new individual is called _____.

## Self test 5

Supply the missing words in the following account of mammalian reproduction.

If (1) has occurred around the time of ovulation, the (2) may encounter a sperm as it passes down the (3) and (4) may occur. The penetration of the (5) by the sperm stimulates the second meiotic division and the secondary oocyte becomes an (6). It usually takes several days for the (7) to travel down the oviduct to the (8), by which time it has already undergone repeated mitotic divisions forming a hollow sphere of cells — the (9).

This becomes embedded in the thickened lining of the uterus (the process is called (10)) and continues its development. The lining of the uterus continues to develop and (11) does not recur. In the ovary, the (12) does not degenerate, but continues to grow.

As pregnancy continues, the embryo develops into a (13) enveloped by protective foetal membranes, the (14), (15) and (16). Some of these membranes combine with the uterine wall to form the (17), which provides the foetus with food and oxygen and removes waste products of the foetal metabolism.

After approximately nine months (the (18) period) the baby is born. The birth process is called (19) and involves strong contractions of the muscular uterine wall which push the baby and the placenta out of the mother's body via the (20) and (21).

During the later stages of pregnancy, the breasts or (22) have been developing under the stimulus of placental (23) and (24) and at parturition are ready to start secreting milk, a process known as (25), to feed the baby.

## Self test 6

1 Copy the figure and complete the labels on the half flower (figure 171).

### 171  A half flower

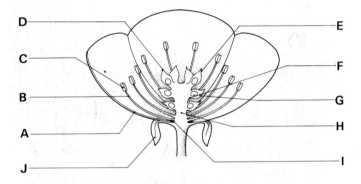

2 State whether this flower is (a) actinomorphic or zygomorphic; (b) sympetalous or polypetalous.
3 Would you expect this flower to be wind or insect-pollinated. Give three reasons for your answer.
4 Distinguish between pollination and fertilisation.
5 List three methods which help to ensure cross-pollination.
6 Name the cell in (a) the anther, (b) the ovule, which undergoes meiotic division.
7 Which part of the flower contributes most to the formation of a fruit?
8 What is the difference between a gynoecium and a carpel?
9 Mammals are dioecious. Do most plants resemble or differ from mammals in this respect? Explain your answer.
10 Figure 172 parts (i)–(v) are diagrams of parts of a flowering plant. They are not drawn to the same

scale. When cells in the root-tip squash of a plant of this species were examined they were found to contain eighteen chromosomes.

For questions (a)–(e) give the number that indicates a structure which
(a) contains a cell which will shortly divide by meiosis,
(b) contains some nuclei with twenty-seven chromosomes,
(c) contains a male gamete,
(d) contains several nuclei, some with nine chromosomes and some with eighteen chomosomes,
(e) contains nuclei with nine chromosomes only.

### 172  Structures in a flowering plant

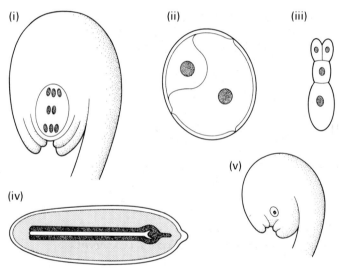

## Self test 7

1 Write down two ways in which external fertilisation in *Hydra* differs from the same process in some other aquatic invertebrates.
2 State three similarities and three differences between the process of reproduction shown by herring and frogs.
3 Summarise sexual reproduction in *Spirogyra*.
4 Name the sex organs of mosses and ferns.
5 Name the structure into which a spore develops in (a) a moss, (b) a fern.

6 How is water involved in the release of spores from (a) a moss, (b) a fern.

7 What may happen to a female cone in (a) year 1, (b) year 2, (c) year 3?

8 Fill in the missing words in the following paragraph:

The male insect tranfers sperm to the female by means of a (1). The sperm may be stored inside the female body in a (2). Thus, eggs may be (3) some time after mating has taken place. Some female insects possess (4) to place eggs under the surface of the soil, etc. The tough shells and internal membranes make insect eggs (5).

9 Write a title for figure 173 and name the structures labelled **A** to **E**

**173   Diagram for question 9**

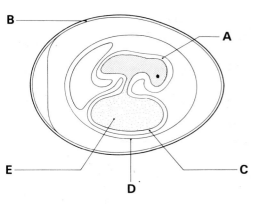

10 Which structure in the diagram in question 9 is particularly concerned with water conservation?

**174   Germinating seeds**

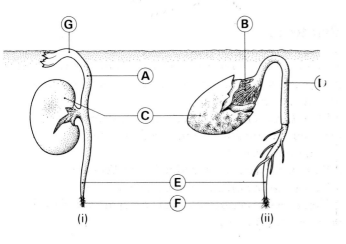

(i)          (ii)

# Self test 8

1 (a) Name the structures labelled **A–F** on diagrams (i) and (ii)(figure 174).

(b) What type of germination is shown by seedling (ii)?

(c) Suggest a reason for the curvature of structure G.

2 (a) List three important conditions for germination.

(b) What is meant by a 'dormant' seed?

(c) Suggest three factors which can cause dormancy.

3 (a) Describe the structure of the cell wall of a parenchyma cell.

(b) How does a collenchyma cell differ from a parenchyma cell?

(c) State one important difference between a parenchyma cell and a lignified cell from the xylem.

**175   LS of a stem apex**

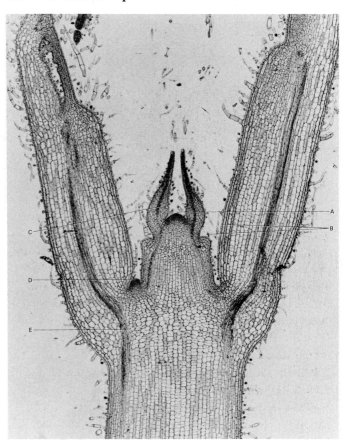

4 What is a pit?

5 Figure 175 is a photomicrograph of part of a stem tip. Name the structures labelled **A, B, C, D** and **E.**

6 Write down three differences between primary and secondary growth.

7 Copy and complete figure 176 to show how new xylem and phloem cells are produced during secondary thickening.

8 Name the structures labelled **A–E** on the photomicrograph, figure 177, and identify the plant organ.

9 From where does a lateral root develop?

10 Complete the gaps in the following short paragraph.

During secondary thickening, the (1) and (2) are gradually replaced by cork. These cells are formed from a (3) just below the epidermis. Cork cells are dead. They prevent the passage of water, (4) and (5) into the stem or root.

**176   Diagram for question 7**

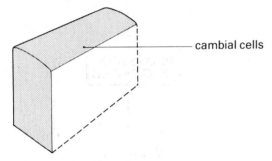

cambial cells

**177   TS of a plant organ**

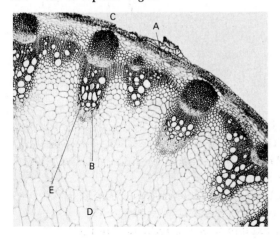

**178   Life-cycle of a bryophyte**

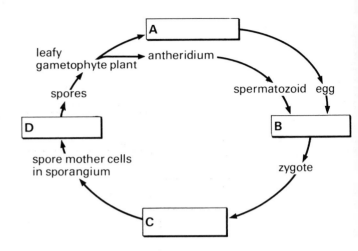

## Self test 9

1 The diagram in figure 178 represents the life-cycle of a bryophyte plant such as a moss or a liverwort. Copy the diagram and

(*a*) write the names of the missing structures clearly in the boxes A and C, and the names of the processes occurring at B and D.

(*b*) Draw a line to separate the diploid and haploid phases.

(*c*) State one difference between bryophytes and ferns.

2 In a similar manner and detail, construct a life-cycle for a fern.

Indicate on your diagram where meiosis occurs.

**179   Young sporophyte on prothallus**

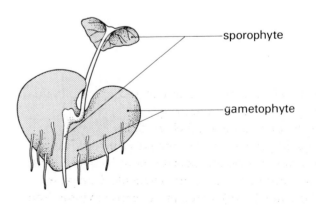

sporophyte

gametophyte

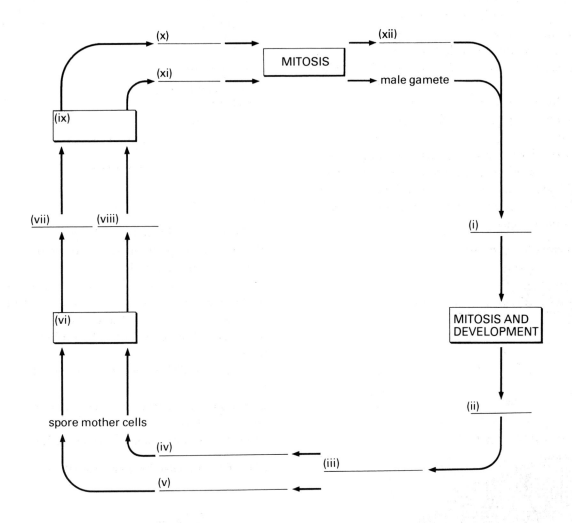

3 Figure 179 shows a young fern sporophyte attached to the prothallus or gametophyte.
Copy the diagram and label the following:
(*a*) haploid generation; (*b*) diploid generation; (*c*) position of male and female reproductive organs.
4 Copy figure 180 into your notebook. Complete it by filling in (i)–(xii) selecting the correct words from the list below:

MITOSIS, flower, egg, female gametophyte, stamen, zygote, MEIOSIS, male gametophyte, megaspore, carpel, MEIOSIS, microspore, diploid sporophyte, pollen sac.
5 (*a*) Briefly explain the difference between a homosporous and heterosporous life-cycle.
(*b*) Briefly explain how the reduction of the gametophyte may be seen as an adaptation to life on land.

(c) Briefly explain how the change to a dominant sporophyte generation may be seen as an adaptation to life on land.

## Self test 10

1 Define (a) cleavage, (b) blastula, (c) gastrulation.
2(a) Name the three cell layers found in the embryos of most multicellular animals.
(b) Give an example of a structure derived from each cell layer by differentiation.
3 List three characteristics common to all larval forms.
4 Suggest two advantages to a species of possessing a larval stage in its life history.
5 (a)Name the labelled parts in the diagram of the tadpole (figure 181).
(b) Suggest an age for this animal and give two reasons for your choice.
(c) What is the food of this tadpole?
(d) Name its main excretory product.

6 Copy, and then fill in the blanks on Figure 182 which summarises hormonal control of amphibian metamorphosis.
7 Give a named example of (a) a holometabolous insect, (b) a hemimetabolous insect.
(c) Briefly explain the difference between the two types of insect.
8 (a) What is ecdysis?
(b) Why is ecdysis important in the development of insects?
(c) Name two glands and two hormones which are involved in ecdysis.
9 Explain the role of the corpora allata in insect metamorphosis.
10 What would you expect to happen if a final instar nymph of *Rhodnius* is decapitated about ten days after a blood meal and joined to an intact first-stage nymph, just emerged from its egg? Give briefly the reasons for your prediction.

**181   Diagram for question 5**

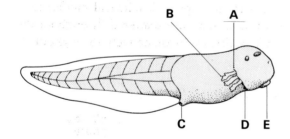

**182   Diagram for question 6**

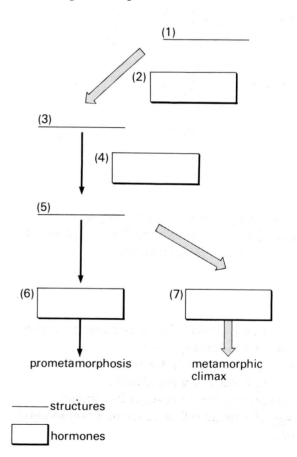

# Section 11 Answers to self tests

## Self test 1

1 (1) nucleus, (2) nuclei, (3) nucleic acid, (4) prophase, (5) thicken, (6) chromatids, (7) nucleus, (8) equator, (9) spindle, (10) centromeres, (11) poles, (12) visible, (13) plate, (14) membrane.
2 **A** chromatid, **B** centriole, **C** spindle fibre, **D** equator.
3 See figure 183.

**183  Answer to question 3**

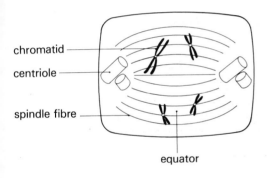

chromatid
centriole
spindle fibre
equator

4 **D** — early prophase, **C** — prophase, **A** — metaphase, **F** — early anaphase, **E** — anaphase, **B** — early telophase, **G** — interphase.

## Self test 2

1 Growth of individuals refers to permanent increase in biomass of a cell or organism.
Population growth refers to the increase in the number of *individuals* in a population.
2 Differentiation refers to changes in form or physiology of a single cell or tissue of a multicellular organism.

Development refers to the change in form, physiology or behaviour of a whole organism as it matures.
3 (*a*) Not usually but wet mass does vary with changes in the amount of water being taken in or given out.
(*b*) Yes, e.g. plants after sowing may increase in size as the seed germinates but there is a loss in dry mass because respiration continues and photosynthesis is not yet established.
4 Interphase.
5 (b).
6 $2.5 \times 10^6$.
7 See figure 184.
8 Five from the following: nutrient supply, temperature, light, water, pH, accumulation of by-products of metabolism, genetic constitution.
9 In plants, growing cells are limited to meristematic areas in stem and root tips and to lateral meristems. Growing cells in animals are scattered throughout the organism. Many tissues divide actively throughout

**184  Answer to question 7**

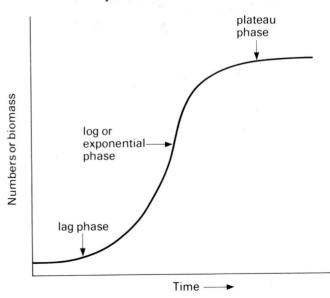

plateau phase

log or exponential phase

lag phase

Numbers or biomass

Time ⟶

life. Other tissues do not divide once differentiated.
10 Division, expansion, differentiation.

## Self test 3

1 *Differences:*
Sexual reproduction: two 'parents' or two types of reproductive cell; offspring genetically different from parents.
Asexual reproduction: one parent; offspring genetically identical to parent.
*Similarity:* New members of the species produced.
2 Three from: abundant food supply, adequate space, favourable temperatures, sufficient moisture.
3 (*a*) In *Paramecium* binary fission is transverse while in *Euglena* it is longitudinal.
(*b*) *Amoeba*, *Schizosaccharomyces pombe*.
4 (i) **A**, (ii) **B** or **C**, (iii) **C**, (iv) **A**.
5 (*a*) Runners grow above ground, suckers below ground.
(*b*) Both are short, vertical stems but in bulbs the leaf bases are swollen with food whereas the base of the stem is swollen in corms.
(*c*) Rhizomes are underground horizontal stems swollen with food along their length. A stem tuber is also underground and horizontal but food is stored at the stem tip only.
6 Perennation involves the means of survival of a plant through seasons in which conditions are disadvantageous. Perennation organs may bring about asexual reproduction *if* they increase the number of plants of the species.
7 (*b*).
8 Compatability, i.e. closely-related subjects. Contact between cambia.
9 Rootstock receives the graft (provides roots and some stem). Scion is grafted onto rootstock.
10 Both involve mitosis. Asexual reproduction is a type of growth but involves increase of population rather than size increase of individual organisms.

## Self test 4

1 Sexual maturation, gametogenesis (meiosis), liberation and dispersal of at least one type of gamete, fertilisation producing a zygote.

2 See figure 185.

**185 Answer to question 2**

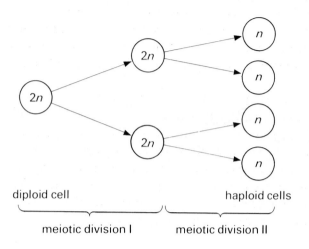

3 Stigma.
4 See figure 186

**186 Answer to question 4**

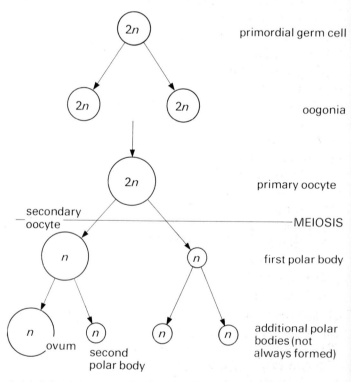

5 (*a*) Megaspore mother cell; (*b*) pollen mother cell.
6 (i) **B**, (ii) **D**, (iii) **F**, (iv) **A**.
7 Heterogametes. They are very different in structure

and size. Isogametes appear identical.

8 Internal fertilisation takes place within the body of the organism. In external fertilisation, both eggs and sperm are liberated from the organisms and fertilisation occurs in a watery environment.

*Advantages:* less wasteful, smaller numbers of gametes required; increased chance of fertilisation; protection for zygote for some period of time; increased chance of survival.

9 (*a*) Hermaphrodite, (*b*) monoecious, (*c*) parthenogenesis.

10 Offspring do not exactly resemble their parents and may be better fitted for the changed conditions. Or, in some organisms, the zygote or early embryo stage is resistant and well-protected and may survive unfavourable conditions in a dormant phase. (Some asexual spores are also fairly resistant.)

## Self test 5

(1) Copulation, coitus or mating
(2) Secondary oocyte
(3) Fallopian tube or oviduct
(4) Fertilisation
(5) Egg membranes
(6) Ovum
(7) Zygote or fertilised egg or developing egg
(8) Uterus
(9) Blastocyst
(10) Implantation
(11) Menstruation
(12) Corpus luteum
(13) Foetus
(14) Chorion ⎫
(15) Amnion ⎬ in any order
(16) Allantois ⎭
(17) Placenta
(18) Gestation
(19) Parturition
(20) Cervix
(21) Vagina
(22) Mammary glands
(23) Oestrogen ⎫
⎬ in either order
(24) Progesterone ⎭
(25) Lactation

## Self test 6

1  **A** petal      **F** ovary
  **B** filament   **G** ovule
  **C** anther     **H** receptacle
  **D** stigma     **I** nectary
  **E** style      **J** sepal

2 (*a*) actinomorphic, (*b*) polypetalous.

3 Insect-pollinated — large petals, nectaries present, easy for insects to alight, small stigma, anthers not very large, etc.

4 Pollination is transfer of pollen from anther to stigma. Fertilisation refers to the fusion of the male and female gametes derived from generative nucleus of pollen cell and egg nucleus of ovule respectively.

5 Three from: protandry, protogyny, unisexual flowers, self-sterility.

6 (*a*) Pollen mother cell, (*b*) megaspore mother cell.

7 Ovary wall (becomes pericarp).

8 The gynoecium is made up of one or more carpels.

9 Differ. Dioecious means that sexes are separate. Most flowers are monoecious (hermaphrodite) though some are dioecious.

10 (*a*) (v), (*b*) (iv), (*c*) (ii), (*d*) (i), (*e*) (iii).

## Self test 7

1 (*a*) Only the male gamete is released by *Hydra* — both gametes are released by many aquatic invertebrates.

(*b*) Early developmental stages of fertilised oocyte occur while attached to parent and thus protected — early stages of development in many invertebrates occur in water.

2 *Similarities:* Both have external fertilisation. Both have a breeding season. Neither provides parental care.

*Differences:* Frogs show courtship behaviour, herring do not. Herring come together in shoals, frogs do not. Frogs: eggs from one female are fertilised by sperm from one male. Herring: eggs may be fertilised by sperm from more than one male. Frogs produce hundreds of eggs. Herring produce thousands of eggs.

3 Two filaments come to lie together. Contents of cells round up. Conjugation tubes form. Cell content

from one filament moves down tube into cells of second filament. Fusion of cell contents and nuclei to form zygote with hard protective wall.

4 Antheridia and archegonia.

5 (a) Protonema (then moss plant); (b) prothallus.

6 (a) Peristome teeth curve inwards in humid conditions and close the capsule. When dry, the teeth curve outwards exposing the opening and releasing the spores.

(b) As the wall of the sporangium dries, the cells lose water and the cells of the annulus are drawn inwards. This causes the thin-walled stomium cells to split. The sporangium splits open; further drying in the annulus cells causes the sporangium to spring closed again, at the same time throwing out the spores.

7 (a) Pollination, (b) fertilisation of the ovule, (c) maturation and release of the seed.

8 (1) penis, (2) spermatheca, (3) fertilised, (4) ovipositors, (5) waterproof.

9 Section through a hen's (bird's) egg.

**A** amniotic fluid, **B** shell, **C** yolk sac, **D** chorion, **E** yolk, **F** allantois.

10 Amnion or amniotic membrane.

middle lamella mainly of calcium pectate.

(b) Collenchyma cells have irregularly thickened primary walls often with extra layers of cellulose at the corners.

(c) One of the following?

a parenchyma cell retains its living contents but a xylem cell is empty (dead or non-living);

a parenchyma cell has a primary cell wall only, a xylem cell has both primary and secondary cell walls

in a parenchyma cell, all the cell dimensions are approximately equal in length. Xylem cells are elongate.

4 A pit is an area of lignified cell wall where no lignin is deposited.

5 **A** Apical meristem  **D** Axillary bud
 **B** Epidermal cells  **E** Procambial strand
 **C** Young leaf

6 *Primary growth*    *Secondary growth*
 apical meristem    lateral meristem
 growth in length    growth in girth
 all tissues formed   vascular tissue formed

7 See figure 187

8 **A** Intervascular   **C** Fibres
  cambium      **D** Pith of parenchyma
 **B** Phloem     **E** Secondary xylem

**187  Answer to question 7**

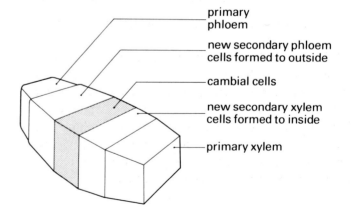

primary phloem
new secondary phloem cells formed to outside
cambial cells
new secondary xylem cells formed to inside
primary xylem

## Self test 8

1 (a) **A** plumule, **B** cotyledons, **C** testa, **D** hypocotyl, **E** radicle, **F** root hairs.

(b) Epigeal germination.

(c) To protect the delicate plumule tip as it breaks through the soil.

2 (a) Water, oxygen, a suitable temperature.

(b) One that, though viable, will not germinate immediately given the conitions listed in 2(a).

(c) Three from the following:

impermeability to water or oxygen;

effects of light — either light sensitive or light hard;

the need for exposure to periods of low temperature;

the need for exposure to a minimum amount of rainfall.

3 (a) A thin primary wall of cellulose microfibrils and hemi-celluloses cemented to adjacent cell walls by a

9 In the pericycle layer within the centre stele.
10 (1) and (2) epidermis and cortex, (3) cork cambium, (4) and (5) gases and microorganisms.


## Self test 9

1 (a) and (b) See figure 188.
(c) In mosses the gametophyte (haploid) generation is dominant but in ferns the sporophyte (diploid) generation is dominant.
2 See figure 189.
3 See figure 190.
4 (i) zygote, (ii) diploid sporophyte, (iii) flower, (iv) carpel (or stamen), (v) stamen (or carpel), (vi) MEIOSIS, (vii) megaspore (or microspore), (viii) microspore (or megaspore), (ix) MITOSIS, (x) female (or male) gametophyte, (xi) male (or female) gametophyte, (xii) egg.
5 (a) An organism with a homosporous life-cycle produces spores which are identical and will germinate to produce a gametophyte bearing male and female reproductive organs.

An organism with a heterosporous life-cycle produces two types of spore of very different sizes. The larger spores give rise to the female gametophyte and the smaller spores to the male gametophyte.
(b) Reduction of the gametophyte makes it less vulnerable to desiccation and mechanical damage especially when it is retained within the sporophyte.

It becomes less dependent on a water environment for fertilisation.
(c) The sporophyte is diploid and a population of such organisms has a greater potential for variation than a haploid population would. Where two sets of hereditary information are present, the effects of harmful characteristics may be masked by dominant advantageous characteristics. This may enable such organisms to survive in changing or extreme conditions such as may be met on land.

**188   Answer to question 1**

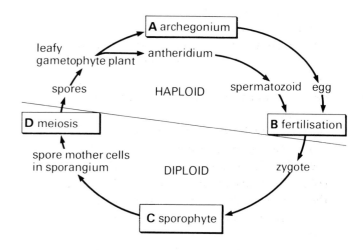

**189   Answer to question 2**

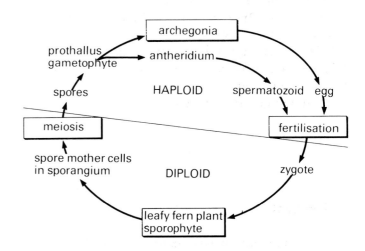

**190   Answer to question 3**

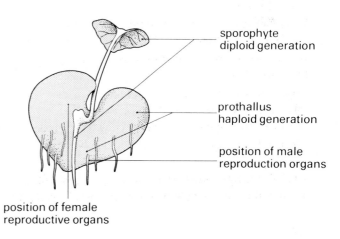

# Self test 10

1 (*a*) The division of the zygote to form a spherical mass of cells.

(*b*) The spherical mass of cells with a central cavity formed during cleavage.

(*c*) Mass movements inwards of groups of cells of the blastula which usually results in the formation of a three-layered gastrula. The inward movement is accompanied by the expansion of other cells to form the outer layer.

2 (*a*) Endoderm, mesoderm, ectoderm.

(*b*) *Endoderm* — thyroid, liver, pancreas, inner wall of gut;

*mesoderm* — sclerotic coat of eye, kidney, gonads, bone, cartilage, muscle, uterus, gut;

*ectoderm* — skin, mouth lining, conjunctiva, cornea, lens, brain and spinal cord, eye vesicles;

3 Structure and physiology different from the adult; capable of living an independent life; sexually immature.

4 Any two of the following:

(*a*) Larva capable of exploiting a different habitat and is not in competition with adults of species.

(*b*) Can play an important part in the dispersal of a species.

(*c*) Larval stage is often concerned mainly with feeding and growth.

5 (*a*) **A** operculum, **B** external gills, **C** anus, **D** sucker, **E** horny-lipped mouth.

(*b*) About seven days — mouth is not present earlier but sucker degenerates after first week. External gills begin to wither after one week and operculum begins to grow. Anus developed after three days.

(*c*) Algae and pond-weed.

(*d*) Ammonia.

6 (1) hypothalamus, (2) thyroid releasing factor (TRF), (3) pituitary, (4) thyroid stimulating hormone (TSH), (5) thyroid, (6) thyroxin (low levels), (7) thyroxin (high levels).

7 One from each of the following:

(*a*) Flies, moths and butterflies, bees and wasps, beetles.

(*b*) Cockroaches, grasshoppers, dragonflies, mayflies and locusts.

(*c*) Holometabolous — hatch from egg totally different in appearance from adult. After several moults an inactive pupa is formed and a radical reorganisation of tissues occurs. Wings develop internally. Pupal case splits to release adult (imago).

Hemimetabolous — hatch from egg resembling adult except for wings and sex organs (nymph). Wings develop externally (gradually). No pupal stage. Adult form after final moult.

8 (*a*) The shedding of old exoskeleton and replacement by a new cuticle (moulting).

(*b*) Allows for growth despite hard exoskeleton.

(*c*) Gland: neurosecretory cells in brain; hormone: brain hormone.

Gland: prothoracic gland; hormone: ecdysone.

9 The corpora allata secrete juvenile hormone. When juvenile hormone is circulating in the blood of an insect, the presence of ecdysone will cause a moult resulting in another immature stage. In the absence of juvenile hormone the ecdysone-induced moult results in the formation of an adult or pupal stage.

10 Both bugs moult. Two adults result — one normal, one 'miniature'. Moulting is induced by hormones of the final instar nymph. No juvenile hormone is yet produced by the newly-hatched nymph so metamorphosis occurs.

# Section 12  Answers to self-assessment questions

1 (*a*) Your graph should look like figure 191.
(*b*) The patterns are very similar for boys and girls until fourteen years is reached. After this, the boys' rate of growth is faster than the girls. This change is associated with puberty, the period of sexual maturation.
2 If individuals were measured just after eating then their recorded mass would be higher than their true biomass. Only after elimination of the waste from their meal could their biomass be more accurately measured. (Similarly, intake of large quantities of liquids would affect measurements.)
3 (*a*) The same technique would involve uprooting the trees every two years. This would disturb their growth and soon cause death.
(*b*) Measurement of height above ground level or width of trunk at a specified height could be used.
4 Problems would include the difficulty of choosing representative individuals. For example, if twenty

trees were all taken from the same small area, they could all be growing faster or slower than those in a different area because of local differences. This problem is usually overcome by designing a system to ensure a random choice from the population. Another problem is that the population is constantly being reduced and this, in itself, could change the growth pattern of other trees by reducing competition, for instance.
5 It is assumed that the characteristic used is directly related to the process being investigated. In this case, that height is directly proportional to biomass.
6 (*a*) Wet mass will vary according to the amounts of water being taken in or given out, whereas dry mass will only vary with changes in the biomass.
(*b*) Your graph should look like figure 192.
(*c*) The pattern of growth shown over these seventy days is very similar for wet mass, dry mass and number of leaves. However, the pattern shown by

**191  Answer to SAQ 1(*a*)**

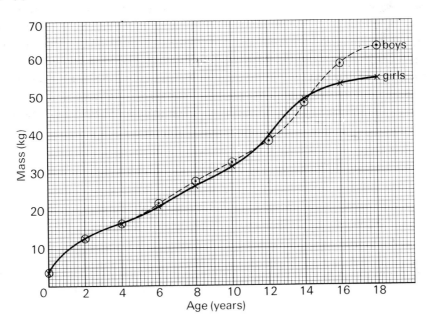

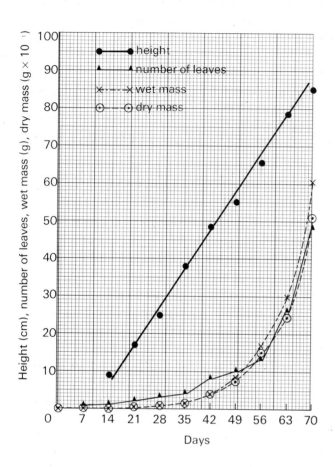

Days

| Mammals | Flowering plants |
|---|---|
| No special regions where growth occurs. Growth may take place throughout the tissues | Growth confined to special regions called meristems |
| Growth is limited. When a mammal has reached maturity growth in size does not usually occur | Growth continues throughout the life of a plant |
| Growth involves cell division but not usually increase in cell size beyond that of the parent cell. (There are exceptions, e.g. eggs) | Growth involves cell division and cell enlargement |

height measurements is quite different. From this evidence, height would appear to be the least reliable measure of growth.

7 (a) Height and mass.

(b) Fresh and dry mass of a sample.

(c) Height and girth of sample.

(d) Mass (living!) of sample numbers of each group.

8 See figure 193.

9 (a) S. pombe is larger than most yeasts and therefore easier to see and count. With a binary fission method of cell division, it is easier to distinguish separate cells.

(b) S. pombe is stated to differ from other yeasts in at least two ways and could be different in many other ways. It is important to appreciate that biologists often work with convenient organisms and these may not always be representative of related organisms and special care must be taken before generalising to different groups of organisms.

10 The assumptions are that every cell divides and that each takes the same time to divide.

11 Graph should look like figure 194.

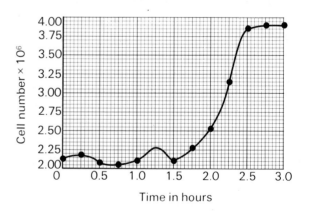

Time in hours

12 (a) Points of difference. The initial population growth is less than the exponential growth shown in figure 23.

After an initial slight increase, there is a decrease in numbers over the first hour and a slight increase in growth rate at 1.25 hours is followed by a decline. (Overall changes are less smooth.)

Rapid growth rate slows down after 2.5 hours.

(b) Similarity. A phase of roughly exponential growth occurs between 1.5 hours and 2.5 hours.

13 The levelling off in growth rate could be due to exhaustion of nutrients required for growth, the inhibiting effect of waste products, or overcrowding due to increased numbers.

14 The curve would flatten out and show no increase after about twenty-two years. (This flattening has begun already at eighteen.) Growth in humans ceases at this age.

15 The curve would flatten out as the oats ripened and growth ceased. If left unharvested the oats, being annual plants, would die.

16 Sigmoid curves. The growth curve of a human being is fairly typical of that for a mammal (though mammals coming to earlier sexual maturity may show a smoother curve). The curve for oats would be typical for annual plants but perennial and biennial plants would show differences in their growth curves.

17 Each year in temperate regions there is an increase in growth rate in spring and summer but this slows in autumn and almost ceases in winter. Leaves produced in spring synthesise food which is assimilated during growth. Deciduous trees shed their leaves in autumn and there is no food for growth. In evergreen trees, lack of light, low temperatures and possible lack of available water will slow growth in winter.

18 (a) The general growth curve shows relatively rapid growth over the first eighteen months, slowing down considerably over the next nine years, followed by another period of rapid growth between the ages of thirteen and seventeen. However, reproductive organs do not grow so quickly initially. There is then a period up to twenty years of age of very rapid growth.

The brain and head grow rapidly for the first four years and relatively slowly for the next sixteen years. Lymphoid tissues grow rapidly up to about twelve years and then actually decrease in size considerably up to the age of twenty years. The general growth curve and that for reproductive organs are both sigmoid in shape.

(b) (i) If the reproductive organs developed any earlier, the individual would be able to reproduce before it could take care of its young.

(ii) The brain develops rapidly during the first months of life which enables a lot of learning to be done — this may aid survival of the young.

(iii) Lymphoid tissue is concerned with resistance to disease and grows rapidly up to puberty, dealing with all the usual diseases to which the young are susceptible. After that time, sufficient immunity has been acquired by the body to defend itself against the most common diseases.

19 Mitotic cell division occurs in both budding and binary fission.

*Differences* (i) In budding, at the time of separation the daughter cell is slightly smaller than the parent cell.

(ii) The bud (partial cell division) occurs *before* mitotic division of nucleus. Binary fission begins with nuclear division, cell division follows.

(iii) The parent cell remains distinguishable in budding and may continue to produce buds. The daughter cells must grow before producing buds. Both cells resulting from binary fission must grow before the next division.

20 *Amoeba* has no clear anterior and posterior as have *Paramecium* and *Euglena*. Transverse fission cuts across the length, longitudinal fission occurs (north–south) along the length.

21 *Paramecium* possesses two nuclei. The meganucleus just constricts and divides (amitotic division) but the micronucleus divides by mitosis.

22 Organelles such as the gullet in *Paramecium* and the reservoir and basal body in *Euglena* must also duplicate and divide. *Amoeba* has little differentiation of its cytoplasm

23 Interstitial cells. These have not become specialised for any one function and can differentiate after dividing to give any type of cell required.

24 An interstitial cell might divide mitotically to produce a group of interstitial cells. Some of these cells might then divide and differentiate to provide other cell types. Gradually, an extension could grow out of the body wall of the parent *Hydra*. By continuous cell growth and division, another *Hydra* would be produced still attached to the parent animal. Food for growth would be supplied by the parent *Hydra*.

25 No, because intersitial cells occur over all regions of the body wall of *Hydra.*

26 Budding in yeast involves the whole organism and only one bud can be produced at a time. Only certain cells of *Hydra* will be involved in bud formation and one animal may have several buds.

27 (*a*) 4, (*b*) 8.

28 (*a*) 4, (*b*) 2.

29 (*a*) Maternal and paternal genetic material is not mixed up, i.e. chromosomes are either black or white.

(*b*) Six out of eight chromosomes are a mixture of black and white. Two remain unchanged.

30 The total chromosome number doubles (i.e. 4 → 8). The chromosome number per cell is reduced (i.e. 4 → 2). The homologous chromosomes exchange material in a random way. The maternal and paternal chromosomes are also randomly divided between the new cells. They have not passed together into a new cell. Each new cell contains a haploid *set* of chromosomes.

31 Primordial germ cells, spermatogonia, oogonia.

32 Secondary spermatocyte, secondary oocyte, first polar body.

33 The first meiotic division *reduces* or halves the number of chromosomes present in each cell (from diploid to haploid) by separating paired chromosomes. The second meiotic division does not alter the chromosome number. (It remains haploid.) In this case, paired chromatids are separated after the centromeres divide.

34 Differences occur during and after meiosis. A primary spermatocyte divides to give two secondary spermatocytes but the primary oocyte divides unevenly to give *one* secondary oocyte and a smaller structure known as a polar body. At second meiotic division, two spermatids result from the secondary spermatocyte but the secondary oocyte produces one large ovum and a smaller polar body. Polar bodies may degenerate. Spermatids then differentiate into spermatozoa. Thus, four spermatozoa result from the division of a primary spermatocyte, but only *one* ovum from the primary oocyte.

35 Primary spermatocytes, primary oocytes.

36 Pollen mother cell, megaspore mother cell.

37 After meiosis, the pollen grain nucleus undergoes further divisions and so does the embryo sac nucleus. Also, the megaspore mother cell gives rise to two similar cells unlike the division of the primary oocyte.

38 Size difference: length of sperm less than diameter of ovum, volume greatly different.

Shape difference: sphere and long thin shape. Much cytoplasm in ovum containing yolk (food reserves). Absence of flagellum in egg. Sperm more easily divided into regions than the ovum. No polar body present in sperm and no acrosome in egg. (Mitochondria are not shown in the egg due to the scale of the drawing. They are present in the cytoplasm.)

39 One gamete needs to be large to contain food reserves to nourish developing embryo after fertilisation. As egg is stationary it can fulfil this role. Motile sperm would require much energy to move food store also.

40 (*a*) To carry genetic information. To travel to the ovum and penetrate it.

(*b*) Head contains DNA which is the genetic information. It possesses an acrosome which carries enzymes that can hydrolyse outer coat of egg. The middle piece is packed with mitochondria to release energy. Tail is constructed like a flagellum to bring about swimming movement and propel the sperm. Sperm contains no non-functional 'extras' which would impede the efficiency of its functioning.

41 The ova are relatively large and represent an 'investment' of food supplies and cytoplasm on the part of the producing organism. They cannot be produced in such vast numbers as sperm, because of demands on food supplies.

Ova are relatively immobile — sperm must 'find' the ova and travel over large distances. Chances of mortality are very great, hence need for large numbers.

Sperm are small and therefore many more can be produced.

42 Removes the problem of finding a mate if self-fertilisation occurs. Even if cross-fertilisation is necessary, this can be achieved with any two animals.

43 Plants are also 'sessile' and chances of reproduction are increased for the same reasons as in 42.

44 Self-fertilisation will not usually produce identical individuals but the chances of variation are reduced and offspring will more closely resemble one another. This may not be of longer-term benefit to the species if conditions change.

45 Worms come together and lie head to tail with segments 9 and 10 opposite the clitellum of the partner. Each worm is enclosed in a separate mucus tube from the opening of the male duct to the clitellum. This prevents mixing of sperm as they pass along the grooves. Worms are attached to each other by secretions from the clitellum and chaetae inserted into the body wall of the partner. Seminal fluid accumulates in the clitellar regions and passes into the spermathecae of the partner. The clitellum secretes material which hardens into a cocoon and this moves towards the anterior of the worm. As it passes the female openings, eggs pass in and sperm are released from the spermathecae. The cocoon is shed from the worm and fertilisation occurs inside the cocoon.

46 If *one* aphid reaches a plant (a good food supply) numbers can rapidly build up. Even if predators are present (e.g. ladybirds) many aphids will survive.

47 (*a*) Increases variation. (*b*) Eggs are a more resistant phase and can remain in a dormant condition until spring when herbaceous plants are again present for food.

48 (*a*) In summer, in conditions of abundant food in pond.
(*b*) If oxygen content of pond drops or cold temperature reduces food supply (i.e. adverse conditions). Fertilised eggs may survive until more favourable food conditions return.

49 Parthenogenesis is usually grouped with sexual methods of reproduction because special sexual structures are involved — eggs produced by ovaries. However, only one parent is involved and individuals may be genetically identical — which links it with asexual reproduction.

50 No. They will be haploid and meiosis will result in an incomplete chromosome complement.

51 **A** spermatogonia, **B** primary spermatocytes, **C** spermatids, **D** spermatozoa

52 Spermatogonia and primary spermatocytes — diploid; spermatids and spermatozoa — haploid.

53 (*a*) Food and oxygen needed for production of spermatozoa — synthesis of new cytoplasm and energy for this. Also removal of waste products of metabolism.
(*b*) Connective tissue surrounding the tubules.

54 Primary oocyte in prophase of first meiotic division.

55 Secondary oocyte (egg is rather imprecise).

56 One polar body.

57 (1) menstruation (2) primary follicle, (3) mature follicle, (4) uterine lining (endometrium) grows, (5) ovulation, (6) corpus luteum, (7) proliferation, (8) menstruation.

58 (*a*)(i) progesterone, (ii) oestrogen.
(*b*) The endometrium of the uterus, pituitary and hypothalamus.

59 Oestrogen and progesterone will inhibit FSH and LH releasing factors. As levels of FSH and LH fall the production of progesterone and oestrogen will also fall. This means that inhibition of FSH and LH production will be removed and their levels will rise again. This pattern will continue to repeat itself.

60 FSH, oestrogen, LH, progesterone.

61 (*a*) Stimulates the growth or repair of the uterine lining.
(*b*) Stimulates the production of LH.
(*c*) Inhibits the production of FSH.

62 (*a*) Rapid growth of the follicle which leads to ovulation.
(*b*) Formation of the corpus luteum.
(*c*) Stimulates the production of progesterone.

63 The inhibitory effect of progesterone and FSH production is removed.

64 From fluids in uterus and fallopian tubes and from the small yolk supply of egg.

65 Endometrium or uterine lining.

66 By proliferation of the endometrium, secretions from the outer layer and increased blood supply containing food.

67 The trophoblast cells.

68 Foetal haemoglobin.

69 10–12%.

70 Foetal blood can carry more oxygen than the maternal blood at a given partial pressure of oxygen.

It will also take up oxygen at partial pressures where maternal blood will give up oxygen — an ideal arrangement.

71 Uterine artery: blood oxygenated. Umbilical artery: blood deoxygenated.

72 This arrangement encourages an efficient transfer of substances between the two series of blood vessels due to the differences in pressure.

73 (a) Nicotine or alcohol or thalidomide.

(b) German measles (Rubella) or syphilis.

74 Progesterone.

75 Transfer suckling stimulus to the pituitary gland.

76 Oxytocin and prolactin.

77 Contains considerably less sugar and more fat. The high fat levels may be important for survival in the cold seas where whales are born, either by liberation of heat energy or by formation of insulation layers in the skin.

78 (a) The developing follicle.

(b) Ovarian tissue.

(c) Progesterone maintains the endometrium in its proliferated state and stops menstruation. It also inhibits FSH and LH production and, hence, further egg release.

(d) The degenerated corpus luteum.

(e) The continued development of the corpus luteum.

79 Chorionic gonadotrophin maintains the corpus luteum during the first few months of pregnancy. It is produced by the developing placenta (allanto-chorion) and its levels are closely associated with that of luteal progesterone.

80 Progesterone is produced by the corpus luteum and placenta. As the corpus luteum degenerates and luteal progesterone drops, the developing placenta causes the subsequent large increase in level.

81 The developing placenta.

82 Oxytocin.

83 (a) Prolactin.

(b) Oestrogen or progesterone or both.

84 (1) oestrogen ⎫
(2) progesterone ⎬ (in any order)
(3) oxytocin ⎭
(4) prolactin

85 (a) high, (b) low, (c) high, (d) high.

86 Foetal blood has a higher affinity for oxygen (see section 4.9.1) and therefore can supply greater amounts of oxygen than could adult blood.

87 After birth the amount of oxyhaemoglobin in the pulmonary artery and right atrium will decrease due to the closing of the foramen ovale and ductus venosus respectively.

88 Anther and filament.

89 Stigma, style and ovary.

90 Receptacle.

91 Interstitial cells.

92 Initially a gelatinous coat, and later a layer of ectoderm cells.

93 Testes generally ripen and release sperm before the ovaries are mature.

94 The oocyte is retained in the body of the *Hydra* until fertilisation and early developmental stages have occurred — only the sperm are released into the water.

95 Embryo develops a resistant chitinous covering and may remain dormant at the bottom of the pond for some time till favourable conditions return.

96 See figure 195.

97 Males and females are prepared to shed their gametes at the same time.

98 Brings male and female into close physical proximity and increases chances of successful fertilisation.

99

| | *Frog* | *Herring* |
|---|---|---|
| (a)(i) | Courtship | No courtship |
| (ii) | Eggs fertilised by one male | Eggs may be fertilised by sperm from more than one male |
| (iii) | Fertilised eggs float in jelly mass. May be attached to plants in water | Fertilised eggs sink |
| (b)(i) | Breeding season | Breeding season |
| (ii) | External fertilisation | External fertilisation |

100 Protects the eggs from bacterial and fungal attack and enables them to float. Focuses sunlight and insulates to allow increase in temperature for more rapid development.

101 From contents of individual cells rounding off.

102 Female gamete is stationary. Male gamete moves.

103 Internal.

104 Resistant zygospores will overwinter and next spring will germinate to reproduce new filaments.

| | Herring | Dogfish |
|---|---|---|
| Breeding season | | Breed throughout the year |
| | Inshore breeding ground | Breed offshore |
| | External fertilisation — sperm released over eggs after release | Internal fertilisation Pairing and copulation lead to |
| | Fertilised eggs sink and attached to substrate | Fertilised eggs enclosed by egg case which is attached to weed |
| | Young drift in surface water | Young migrate to deeper water |
| | Thousands of eggs released | About 100 eggs per year |

105 (a) *Fucus* has external fertilisation. *Spirogyra* has internal fertilisation.

(b) *Fucus* produces specialised gametes in reproductive organs, oogonia and antheridia. *Spirogyra* has no specialised reproductive structures. Each cell of the filament can act as a gamete.

(c) The male gametes of *Fucus* are flagellated; those of *Spirogyra* are amoeboid.

(d) The zygote of *Fucus* grows into a new plant straight away. The zygospore of *Spirogyra* is a resting stage.

106 Zygospore of *Spirogyra* is surrounded by a thick wall and contains oil as a food store. It is a resistant stage which falls to the bottom of the pond and remains dormant until favourable conditions arise. *Fucus* zygote is surrounded by a gelatinous membrane. It then acquires a cell wall and germinates immediately.

107 (a) The gametophyte requires water.

(b) Water is needed for the motile sperm to be able to reach and fertilise the egg.

108 Not tied to water, plants can populate a much wider variety of habitats.

109 Mammals protect gametes and zygote from desiccation in the following ways:

(a) Male and female secrete a fluid medium for the gametes. Fertilisation is internal.

(b) Embryo is retained inside uterus of female (egg or pouch). Extra embryonic membranes to help water conservation.

110 Insects prevent desiccation in gametes and the developing embryo by:

(a) Internal fertilisation.

(b) (i) Waterproof shell surrounding ovum (sometimes eggs are also surrounded by egg pod); (ii) ovipositors to place eggs in humid environment.

111 Seeds which can lie dormant for a long time can put off germination until suitable conditions occur. This increases their chances of survival. It is of particular advantage when, for example, a long spell of unsuitable weather occurs.

112 Seed coat or testa.

113 The testa may be broken down by water gradually seeping into the seed or by the action of microorganisms.

114 Small seeds will only have a small food reserve. Therefore it is necessary that they start to photosynthesise very soon after germination. If they germinate too deep in the soil they might use up their small food reserves before penetrating to the surface. The light requirement ensures that they only germinate near the surface.

115 Ploughing may bring the seeds into regions more favourable to germination — $O_2$ availability will be greater, temperature may be higher and light will be available for light-sensitive seeds.

116 Such seeds are likely to be produced in regions of the world where there is a cold season. The requirement ensures that the seeds remain dormant during the cold winter and only germinate in the following spring. It prevents premature germination in a mild autumn.

117 Such seeds may remain dormant in dry conditions and only germinate after a heavy shower of rain. This will produce sufficient water to wash away inhibitors from the seed if present, break down the testa and allow the seed to germinate and complete its life-cycle within a short time.

118 It causes the testa to swell up and split, thus allowing emergence of the radicle.

119 During germination, starch levels in the seed drop. At the same time, levels of amylase rise. Amylase is the enzyme responsible for breaking down the starch into soluble sugars which are used by the developing embryo.

120 It is insoluble and therefore does not affect water movement by osmosis.

121 Starch is converted into sugars, fats into fatty acids and glycerol and proteins into amino acids.

122 The rise in amylase levels during germination must be due to the synthesis of molecules of the enzyme. This synthesis requires energy. Energy is released during respiration in which oxygen is necessary.

123 The food reserves are broken down during respiration to $CO_2$ which is evolved and water which is eliminated during dry-mass measurements. There is no complementary synthesis of food until photosynthesis begins. Therefore, there is an overall loss in mass.

124 Vascular tissue is central in a root. In a stem it is arranged in bundles toward the periphery.

125 **A** apical meristem, **B** epidermal cells, **C** young leaf, **D** axillary bud, **E** procambial strand

126 (a) Secondary growth occurs at lateral, not apical meristem; it results in girth, not length, changes; and it is largely concerned with vascular tissue (apart from cork formation, dealt with later).

(b) The primary phloem cells are crushed and flattened by the pressure from secondary growth tissue. Primary xylem cells are less affected and usually remain intact.

127 Parenchyma cells act as a nutrient pathway connecting the living cells in the outer layer with those in the centre of the plant.

128 Five years.

129 The lateral root develops in the pericycle layer within the stele at the centre of the root.

130 (a) meiosis, (b) mitosis.

131 Gametes are always haploid. Zygotes are always diploid.

132 (i) *n*, (ii) 2*n*, (iii) 2*n*, (iv) *n*, (v) *n*.

133 (a) The higher plant life-cycle involves an alternating asexual (spore-producing) and sexual (gamete-producing) phase. In *Spirogyra* there is no regular alternation of these phases.

(b) There is a complex, multicellular diploid phase, the sporophyte. In *Spirogyra,* the diploid phase is a one-celled stage, the zygote.

134 *Spirogyra*

(a) One-celled.

(b) Undifferentiated.

(c) Cannot photosynthesise.

*A moss*

(a) Multicellular.

(b) Differentiation into stem, spore capsule and 'foot'.

(c) Limited photosynthesis.

(d) Mainly dependent on gametophyte for nutrition.

*A fern*

(a) Multi-celled, complex structure.

(b) Differentiated into stem, rhizome, leaves and roots.

(c) Able to photosynthesise.

(d) Becomes independent of gametophyte for nutrition.

135 Sporophyte. This is the spore-producing stage.

136 Gametophyte.

137 (a) sporangium, (b) anther and ovule.

138 (a) Archegonium on the leafy plant of the gametophyte generation.

(b) Archegonium in the female gametophyte which is retained within the megaspore.

139 (a) ovule, (b) anther.

140 The fragile gametophyte is protected against desiccation and mechanical damage by the layers of the ovule (integuments, ovary wall, etc.) or the resistant wall of the pollen grain.

141 (a) spores, (b) spores, (c) seeds.

142 (a) Seeds are larger than spores and contain greater food reserves.

(b) Seeds are protected by a thick testa.

(c) Seeds may be modified in various ways to aid dispersal in space (wings, hooks, etc.). Various factors in seeds control dormancy — this aids dispersal in time. The embryo in seeds is well advanced in development giving a greater chance of survival on germination.

143 In mammals a diploid organism produces haploid gametes *by meiosis*. Fertilisation between pairs of gametes produces a zygote which develops into a diploid organism.

In angiosperms a diploid organism produces haploid spores (pollen grain and megaspore) by meiosis. These give rise to haploid gametophytes which produce gametes *by mitosis*. Fertilisation between pairs of gametes produces a zygote which develops nto a diploid organism.

44 Cleavage establishes a normal relationship between the nucleus (DNA) and the cytoplasm whose activities it regulates.

45 Even before fertilisation the egg has well-developed differences in cytoplasm of different regions. Cleavage produces cells that have different cytoplasmic constituents; different cytoplasm will affect the identical nuclei in different ways and so allowing different structures to be formed.

46 (a) Gut (inner wall from endoderm and smooth muscle from mesoderm).
(b) Eye (sclerotic coat from mesoderm and conjunctiva, cornea, lens, etc. from ectoderm).

47 The characteristics mean that a larva is capable of exploiting a different habitat and is usually not in direct competition with adults of its own species for food.

148 (a) Dispersal of species.
(b) Building up of food store or biomass (growth).

149 (a) Larva (external gills, excretes ammonia and has tail) is very different to the adult (lungs, excretes urea and has four limbs).
(b) Larva is an aquatic herbivore and adult a terrestrial carnivore.
(c) Larva is incapable of reproduction.

150 Young tadpoles are herbivores. A herbivorous diet requires a greater bulk and is more difficult to digest and therefore a longer gut is required. Older tadpoles change to a carnivorous diet which is more easily digested and so a shorter gut will suffice.

151 Relative proportions of enzymes present will alter. Some gut flora essential to digestion of cellulose may be lost.

152 There is less oxygen per unit volume in water than in air.

153 Ammonia is toxic. Aquatic animals have no water shortage and they can keep ammonia very dilute and excrete a watery urine in copious amounts. Land animals must conserve water and therefore convert ammonia into a less toxic product, urea, which can be excreted in a much higher concentration and with less water loss.

154 Shortening of gut and development of internal gills. (Frogs injected are, after nine days, developed to show structure of four weeks.)

155 Associated with change of diet, horny lips were suited for herbivorous diet, larger mouth required to acccommodate live food as a carnivore.

156 The tail which is being reabsorbed.

157 In young tadpoles, the thyroid gland is small and relatively undeveloped. The thyroid gland grows and actively begins to secrete its hormones and these hormones circulating in the blood bring about metamorphic change shown by tadpole 2.

158 Yes. Removal if the thyroid inhibits metamorphosis which demonstrates the dependence of the process on this endocrine gland. Thyroid extract speeds up metamorphosis even when the gland has been removed showing it is the hormone that is directly responsible for metamorphosis.

159 The fact that extract of sheep's thyroid brings about metamorphosis of amphibia suggests that the hormones must be chemically very similar.

160 The early stages of metamorphic change require low doses of thyroxin. Much greater amounts of thyroxin are required for metamorphic climax.

161 This is supported by the appearance of the thyroid gland (as described in investigation B) which develops greatly before metamorphic climax.

162 In normal circumstances the pituitary produces small amounts of TSH without stimulation from the brain (via TRF). The level of TSH is sufficient to stimulate only low levels of thyroxin which cause

**196   Answer to SAQ 163**

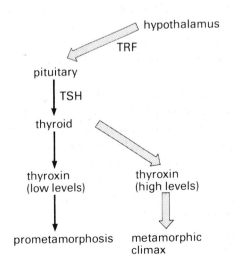

prometamorphosis. However, for the higher levels of thyroxin needed for metamorphic climax, pituitary production of TSH is only raised sufficiently by stimulation of TRF from the hypothalamus.

163 See figure 196.

164 Five instars.

165 Ecdysis takes place and increase in size is possible while the new cuticle is soft. The rapid increase in mass in *Notonecta* is probably produced by the swallowing of water which causes the insect to swell and stretch the cuticle.

166 The rapid increase in mass is due to the uptake of water which is not part of the organism's biomass and therefore does not contribute towards growth.

167 For true growth to occur (permanent increase in biomass), the water gained must be gradually lost and replaced by assimilated food.

168 Investigation 1 shows that insects without a head *can* moult *if a certain critical time has elapsed* since a blood meal. This suggests the possibility that a hormone must reach a certain threshold level before moulting can occur. Or, the hormone may not actually be produced until nine days after feeding.

169 Investigation 2 lends weight to the idea that a hormone is involved as the link between the two insects is via the circulating blood.

170 Kopec had established that some kind of hormone concerned with development was secreted by the brain, but Investigation 3 suggests that both head and thorax play some part in control of development. However, neither head nor thorax *alone* can bring about moulting.

171 The first-instar nymph has produced a hormone that prevents the appearance of the adult characteristics in the fifth instar.

172 After the moult, another *Rhodnius* nymph not an adult is produced.

173 The corpora allata are endocrine glands that secrete the hormone that inhibits the expression of the adult characteristics and maintains the juvenile features.

174 (*a*) ecdysone, (*b*) juvenile hormone.

175 (1) 'brain hormone', (2) ecdysone, (3) juvenile hormone.

176 *Rhodnius* development involves two separate elements, moulting and the subsequent appearance of adult features. Moulting is controlled by the hormone ecdysone. Juvenile hormone is produced by the corpora allata in instars 1–4 and this prevents adult characters from being expressed after the moult. Instar 5 has ecdysone *only* circulating in its blood. This brings about moulting and the absence of juvenile hormone means that adult features can appear.

# Index